SECOND WIND

SECOND WIND

*Words and Art
of Hope and Resilience*

Editors, Kate Aver Avraham
and Melody Culver

Cover Design: Tor Anderson

Cover Painting: Sarah Bianco,
"We Couldn't Have Done It Without Us"
(full painting on pages 62-63)

If you enjoy the art or writing, see "About the Artists
and Authors" section and feel free to look them up!

PERMISSIONS

Ellen Bass, "Any Common Desolation" reprinted with permission of Permissions Co. LLC on behalf of coppercanyonpress.org.

Gail Brenner, "The Lean Years" a version previously published in *phren-Z*.

Pamela Eakins, "Three of Wind" image by permission of US Games, Inc.

Diane Frank, all poems from the upcoming *While Listening to the Enigma Variations,* Glass Lyre Press.

Gail Newman, "I Came Into the World," "Laundry, 1952," and "The Journey" from *Blood Memory,* Marsh Hawk Press.

Maggie Paul, "After Machado" and "Iris" from *Borrowed World,* Hummingbird Press; "To Walk Among the Living" and "Love Poem" from *Scrimshaw,* Hummingbird Press.

Patrice Vecchione, "And If I Don't Write?" from *My Shouting, Shattered, Whispering Voice,* Seven Stories Press.

*For all the generous
and creative souls
who made this book possible*

In Praise of What Lies Between Us

Bless every space between,
every spore-carrying
wing-whipped
cry-pierced
sun-lit
space that lies
from frond to frond
rock to stream
mouth to ear
star to skin.
Bless the diaphragm
that throws the voice
and the eardrum that catches it.
Bless the original fire
of the universe
and the farthest star.
Bless the hyphal tips
of mycelium digesting
the dead to make a bridge
of life between oak and alder.

Bless the space between
and bless every clear-hearted endeavor
to hold each other dear across distance.
Bless the print and scat and scrape readers
who close the space
between yesterday and today.
Bless the chalk writers and sand sketchers.
Bless the signal fire keepers
and ghost repeaters.
Bless the watchers and listeners.
Bless the menders with their bags
of thread and wire, patches and glue.
Bless the ancestors and descendants
and every strand of DNA strung between.
Bless every humming thread
from then to now to when
from there to here to where
from me to you to who.

Finn Gratton

CONTENTS

CONTENTS

Preface 1

Grief and resilience live together. –Michelle Obama, *Becoming*

Second Wind began as a vision, a dream amidst my own grief over what was happening in the world. It was during the early days of the pandemic, when life as we had known it was almost completely shut down and we were sheltering in place. Locally and globally, people were losing loved ones, incomes, unable to pay rent or buy enough food for their families. This vision of a way to help kept nudging me. I was one of the lucky ones who did not have to struggle financially and had a safe, secure home.

Nudge...nudge...nudge. I woke up one bright blue early spring morning and knew I had to put the vision into action. I also knew exactly who I would approach to take the journey with me . . . my big-hearted, savvy soul sister and partner in crime, Melody. It didn't take any nudging at all to bring her on board, and off we went . . .

The journey toward this book has been filled with profound reciprocity. For every day we worked, we also received so much affirmation, appreciation and support from everyone involved. Over and over we got our own "second wind," our own hope and resilience from the outpouring of encouragement and love from contributors.

And this anthology in itself seems to answer your question of what to do in difficult times . . . you gather friends, skills and possibilities and create something that can tilt the balance of concerns for good, and for that alone I am grateful. –Ratna Sturz, contributor

My heartfelt gratitude to ALL of you. Now, may the journey we have been on together emanate into the world like ripples in a pond, to offer hope, healing and financial assistance to those in our community most affected by the pandemic and the fires.

Whatever you can do, begin it. Boldness has genius,
power and magic in it.   –Johann von Goethe

Kate Aver Avraham

Preface 2

While sheltering in place, emotional states during the early days of the pandemic felt similar to the initial stages of grieving. In the midst of denial and anger, swinging through overreaction and feelings of, urgency and melancholy, there was an occasional glimpse, an errant thought while doing something else: *This is a way it could be different. This is how I could choose to be.* A friend said, "The shock provides an opening, a glimpse of soul possibility." The window may close again, curtained by the routine demands of life and a slew of conflicting emotions, but the flicker of possibility is there, shining.

I felt aimless, unmoored, without structure, the work I'd been doing for more than a decade ended. Bargaining set in, and distraction, and the quest for "normal." But attempts at normal—a trip to the craft store or going to a restaurant with outdoor seating—raised low-lying anxiety to a higher level and spurred a quick return to the safety and relief of my home nest.

Like others, I went in and out of the next stage, depression and sadness. Some days it lay thick like a gray dishrag, blunting emotion and dampening energy. Once in a while, mysteriously, it lifted and I could see to the horizon line of "when all this is over," only later to realize that it may not be "all over," ever, that our lives have morphed into something unknown. Old patterns and habits were no longer valid, expectations were cancelled. What now? What to do without the companionship of friends and visits with family? How to fill the long hours without work? Craft supplies came out of closets, tabletops filled with projects, baskets of yarn sat next to the couch. I read stacks of books, trading with neighbors and friends. I put on a few pounds.

Then my soul sister Kate had the inspired idea to put together an anthology of writers and artists, all talking about and showing what gets them through these stages and these times. The book would showcase their creativity and gather words of hope and possibility from their good hearts and varied and precious minds. Possibly, such a book could be of help to others. Certainly, it would be a worthy project. And we would donate profits to the Community Foundation of Santa Cruz County's COVID-19 Response Fund.

While I, like most of us, continue to cycle through different forms and layers of denial, anger, bargaining and depression, helping create this anthology has enabled movement toward acceptance. Not assent to ongoing uncertainty forever, not acceptance of this stultified world or the political insanity, but acknowledgement that I had a focus. *This is your mission, should you choose to accept it.* I had something to mull over and plan for, a reason to get up in the morning. I felt like a seabird emerging from dark waters; I could float on the days.

Then came the rare and incredibly beautiful lightning storm that lit massive fires, knocking the Central Coast of California into a Mad Max world of orange skies and flying ash and evacuations, and spreading throughout the state and onward. Many could not breathe well. People were evacuated, lost loved ones, treasured belongings, their homes. Still sheltering, we contended with a fresh round of emotional ups and downs.

But oh, the remarkable artistry and writing Kate and I have been privileged and grateful to read and appreciate! Wry, real, imaginative, heartfelt, anguished, urgent, filled with beauty and solace that flipped my heart over. The drumming backbeat of fear and anxiety turned inside out and became a steady heartbeat.

When looking through a window screen, we can focus on the mesh near our eyes, seeing only little squares, or we can look through it, past it, to a larger perspective . . . it takes a simple adjustment, relaxing the eyes and brain. Our close mesh of safety restrictions is still here, and now I can see through to focus on the expansive outer world where plants keep growing and discoveries are still made and the stars continue to turn in their circuits when viewed from the hammock on sleepless nights.

I can see past the heart-pumping news and calamities to acknowledge and appreciate: Most people are fundamentally thoughtful and kind and generous and caring. The minor-key tension resolves to the relief of a major chord. *We can choose to adjust. We can choose to change.* Every one of us has that power.

Our possibilities depend on our ability to hear and recognize them for what they are: the quiet voices of our souls, suggesting what could be next. With deep listening, hope and resilience, we can do this; we *are* doing this, alone and together.

Melody Culver
October 2020

$\mathcal{A}$cknowledgements

To Sarah Bianco, for the generous use
of her painting on the cover

to Tor Anderson, graphic designer extraordinaire

to the anonymous donor (from your travel fund)

and to Blue Moon Creations,

our heartfelt gratitude.

–KAA & MC

HEARTACHE
in the
LAND

Kitchen Table

Life
in a tiny terrarium
in this moment outside time

tendrils reaching
long leaves curling
spikes and dirt

Life
orbits the curvy
blue bowl of it

music and silence
conversations

steam from our teapot
the only weather

Anne Ylvisaker

Quarantined

Before, each morning
came gift-wrapped,
tied by a ribbon of light
on a breaking wave,
specially delivered
to the shoreline
to meet me walking.

Deep breaths
in time to ocean's pulse . . .
pace slowing
matching heartbeat.

This morning,
I awake in a panic . . .
that ribbon of light,
a police tape
around the front door
to keep me from drowning
in a viral tsunami.

I listen to the birds.

Dan Phillips

Sanctuary–Mixed Media, Nancy Jones
Hurricane House, Fall 2019

Corona

When all this ends, who will be left, or right, or missing?
Who will bear the gaunt eye and the hollow belly
the hope and the pearl? Of great price, I'm sure.
I am wondering these things, trying not to shout, as I sip my tea
as I stare into the hollow of my computer screen, this crazy dream.
Trying not to look at so, so much, in and out of touch.
There are things I want to know and do not want to know.
How the wind blows, say, and what it might carry.
The seeds of love, or a poison so bleak
as to germinate the further dying
of a planet on the brink of its own brutal demise.
My eyes, the lies, sorrowing, turning away
or so cruelly wise I cannot deny what I think I know I see.
About you and your heart, about me
and the small bird of fear that is crouched
crazed, in the wild nest of the mind.
Has this been planned, as some say? Conspiracy!
This unimaginable tragedy, this precise, well-crafted genocide.
A world taken down. I'm just trying to comprehend
is that too much to ask, to take to task?
My solitary confinement, my needing here to dwell
to avoid another kind of hell. The lungs full
or worse, this curse, a body on a stretcher, no mourners
time will tell. Having it better than some, most.
The "do not enter" sign posted, right there:
Careful, Danger! Beware!
I am a fickle host, shunning my guests. I need to rest
I need to rise, like the sun, finally
after so much drear and rain, after another cold winter
grateful to be inside.

Lo! Finally, again, another spring!
I hide. But look. For you, a truth
something absolute where there is only this:
The wind, finally warm, a gentle kiss.
And my face, turning toward the light.
Even in the night, I lay, I wait, I ask but do not assume
not sure who else is listening, just there in the next room.
If it be God or cruel jest
unsure like all the rest. The walls have ears!
Calling in my soul, hoping to be whole, certainly.
When nothing is certain and yet. I make these words
absurd as this whole situation seems to get.
What is to become of me, we ask?
Glorifying a past that will no longer be.
Our way. Of life.
Simple pleasures. A chance to talk close. A cup of tea.
The pressing of body to body, free.
In love. So I write you this. My SOS.
A small poetic kiss. Good morning, world,
dangerous as you may threaten to be.
Here is a little sorrowed love song from me.
I see you, through the window, and still, still
I bow, I pray, I offer my heart
to this full, empty, chaotic, glorious
tentative passage of day.

Johanna Courtleigh

Sheltering

Afternoon
utterly still
hiss of steam
the iron lifts
from the cloth
a long exhale
old ironing board
sturdy, dependable
heap of fresh-washed
fabric on the bed

Slow glide of heat
over bright prints
sun-yellow orchids
pale plumeria, crimson
hibiscus, verdant
philodendron bloom
on a field of blue
deeper than an
island lagoon
as if paradise
were here

Down south
clerks still
at their posts
in the grocery mart
finally get
one mask each
ill-fitting, flimsy
my son reports
while managers
take for themselves
the large cache
of disposables

Now the swaths
of fabric pressed
and folded
still warm
are placed
one by one in a
tissue-lined box
something I can
do to keep busy
something maybe
somehow
to save his life

Gail Brenner
4/15/2020

Pause

In still moments
sounds of *Pause*
float up
aromatic and soothing
as steam from hot soup

I suggest to myself,
Step back
       from circles of activity that deplete you
Refrain
       from saying automatic *yes* or *no*
Engage fully
       When you stare into the mirror of authenticity and
Smile

Pause lends a perch
       to survey the larger landscape.
Pause gives eyes
       to penetrate where I truly belong.
Pause. Pause. Pause.

Can I be
a freshly birthed person
in a newly created
environment?

Masks
social distancing.
I go out alone
see almost no one
barely step into a store.

Life controlled
by others
no guests allowed,
no friends
to enter my door
for conversation
pause expectation
pause past thinking,
pause past roles and relationships

Plans for my life shift
without my consent.
Pause.
Discover what awaits.

Ratna Jennifer Sturz
July 29, 2020

Wonder Not Worry

My friends do the fretting. They worry about which of the three Cs will get me first. Cancer and chemo were obvious contenders, and now I have to fight with COVID. It's a race I've been registered for without choice. The proverbial tortoise and hare with noses at the starting line. The third entrant, a cheetah, saunters about, nonchalant. My friends make wagers. The smart ones, with financial brains, bet on the speed of the cheetah who can race around the world twice before the others move. The empaths side with the tortoise, on whose back I ride. Nobody bets on the hare, whose history as a loser proceeds it.

When the gun is fired, the hare and cheetah bolt, having been shot at before, and outrun the bullets. The tortoise and I continue a journey we've been on together for months. We stop to listen to the memories of extinct birds echoed by mockingbirds. We inhale the pennyroyal and feverfew. We pay attention to where we are, where we've been, where were headed.

The others are gone. It doesn't matter. We have different finish lines. My friends watch. Bounce on the balls of their feet. Hold their breath. Chew their fingernails. Worry about their wagers. The tortoise and I ignore their three Cs. Are in pursuit of our own. We are distracted by the wonders along the pathway.

Gather compassion. Hunt for community. Celebrate every inhale, every exhale.

We wonder what's next.

Jory Post

Zoom Meditations: Variations on a Theme

Zoom I

Walking through my neighborhood in the early evening, I love glancing inside people's homes. Curtains are not yet closed, and my eyes are pulled to the warm glow inside. Golden light against night's arrival feels modern and ancient. My eyes are drawn to linger. It has always felt heartwarming but edgy to look inside.

It is April 2020, the pandemic times, and I am meeting people on Zoom. Unlike the evening walks through the neighborhood, my direct gaze is accepted and welcomed. I see inside homes: with the morning light, afternoon brightness, lamp-lit evenings. Interior details are framed. A stuffed penguin sits behind Lila. Debra's wall art is an eighteenth-century Chinese presentation fan. Holly zooms from the red-walled bedroom her son painted years before he left for England, and Janet sits with her giant, carefree dog sprawled beside her. Each a stunning portrait.

I confess a visceral thrill as each person signs into their rectangle box. *There they are!* says my internal voice. *They are alive and sheltered just like me.*

Everyone stares at the screen unconsciously while adjusting sound and video, then settles into a comfy seated position. Random sounds emanate from each home. The presence of spring birdsong—is it coming from my house or theirs? We are all still sharing the same sky.

There is an awkwardness to the intimacy here.

Maybe we can all sniff vulnerability through our computer screen. Uncertainty has rattled us all. It is not clear in the moment who is holding it together and who is falling apart, whose heart is tender, who is worried about loved ones, who is afraid, who is lonely, whose lives teeter with insecurity, who is listening to too much news, who is crying, which hearts are broken. Who has gone deeply inside for refuge? Whose anxiety is caged or running wild?

Glowing images from each room belie the truth that none of us knows when this will end, nor how it will end. None among us holds the future. Reality has shifted for all of us, as quickly as turning a Zoom screen on and off. People are suffering deeply. The growing discomfort with the new reality is palpable. We all feel this.

Zoom II

In the virtual world, I never know where to rest my eyes. I have heard that staring at the green light at the top center of the screen is the best way to connect with others, but my eyes search insistently for the eyes of the speaker, regardless if they are bottom left or middle right on my screen.

Vigilant, I stay perched for the possible moment our eyes lock, when my whole body feels that moment of human recognition, cognition, connection. My longing is satisfied. No matter what words are being said, I can sense they really see me and they know they are being seen.

Eye contact is medicine.

This is what we look like when life as we know it has stopped.

Zoom III

I position myself in front of a blank white wall. I love its starkness. Just me plain and simple on the screen. Like a sole stark figure in a cold winter landscape of snowy whiteness.

Off camera is different. In front of me, the detritus of my life: unfinished paintings on my easel and the floor. Turquoise curtains hide washer and dryer and a pile of cloth napkins and rags, testimony to my pandemic commitment to stop using paper towels. Aside the laundry area are the doors to the pantry, so overstuffed they barely close. The mess of daily life surrounds me.

Here in this strange new world, I meet the gaze of beloved friends, family and students whose bodies and hearts I have watched for years as they stretched with life and aged with time.

Their spirits fire a spark inside my heart.

They are my new heroes, those whose lives I follow, whose struggles and joys with the pandemic compel and inspire me. There is awe in these honest faces living through each unsettling day.

Zoom IV

Join Zoom meeting
Leave Zoom meeting
Chat
Speaker view
Gallery view
Allow
Allow computer with audio
Allow audio with computer
Breakout room
You are muted
Unmute yourself

Zoom wedding
Zoom funeral
Zoom bris
Zoom birthday party
Zoom bridal shower
Zoom writing classes, art classes, cooking, reading groups, dinner parties
Zoom family gathering
You are muted
Unmute yourself

Zoom dog training
Zoom doctor meeting
Zoom instructions on how to clean hearing aids
Zoom business meetings
Zoom therapy
Zoom poetry reading
You are muted
Unmute yourself

Zoom V

Rectangles

My son Kobi lives in a rectangular apartment on the eleventh floor of a densely packed city-state with 6 million people. He has been sheltered in place in Singapore, on the tip of the southern Malaysian peninsula. COVID arrived and stopped life there before coming here to the US.

I zoom-visit him, each of us in our small rectangles.

Rectangles are a trusted, familiar shape. They are honest, rational, practical, grounded. Perfect to contain the ache of the heart.

Recently, I read a Buddhist story in *The Hidden Lamp*.

Crying in deep despair, an earnest meditation student asked her teacher, Sisho Maylie Scott*, "I've worked so hard to transform this crippling loneliness, I can neither shake it nor live with it. Can you help me?"

I could relate to this student's plaintive human cry for relief.

Holding the student in a steady gaze and offering her confident smile, Maylie ended the conversation with this one line, "Please don't ever think anything is out of place."

Nothing is out of place. Nothing is out of place.

Karen Zelin

*Maylie Scott, American Buddhist teacher and social worker, 1935-2011

Time Drops its Mask

We tumble into day
forgetting our sleep and plunge
ourselves into the doing.
But now the pandemic has careened us
into sheltering in place and
I, living alone,
fill my bare living room with paintings and tubes of color,
painting the rhythms of my journey from deeper places.
This interior life now navigates my orientation.

Time drops its mask of linearity,
becomes a deeper engagement with myself,
the clarity of this opportunity to stop the world,

an offering,

while in my heart, humanity, the suffering, loss and grief,
the courage,
the long shadowy fears of uncertainty
fill my awareness, and walk with me.

Here, and solitary, I am having a different experience,
sinking more deeply into this Earth, this spring,
the bright green bursting out
of bare limbs,
the red of roses opening through
their fragrance,
little birds in their humming
weave together the garden,
and in early morning hours
the starry alignment,

orbs of light, Mars, Saturn and Jupiter,
a bridge in the sky I could walk upon.
Pluto, the invisible, there too,
a silent siren,
phoenix of transformation,

an astrological signature
of this pandemic, bringing out
all the shadowy aspects that infect us,
stunning us into new ways of living.

This morning I make tea at 3 am and sit upon my bed to write,
attuning to the throbbing heart of renewal,
and as if standing upon a tall plateau, I look over
the landscape and see these things,
see the view of this world, this humanity all intertwined
in one huge weaving.

Most of all,
in this morning of hushed darkness,
I see the root beer-scented iris
that took to blooming in the starry night under
the dark round of new moon,

its mystery
silently revealing the secrets and intelligence of this
our Earth.

Susan Heinz
April 2020

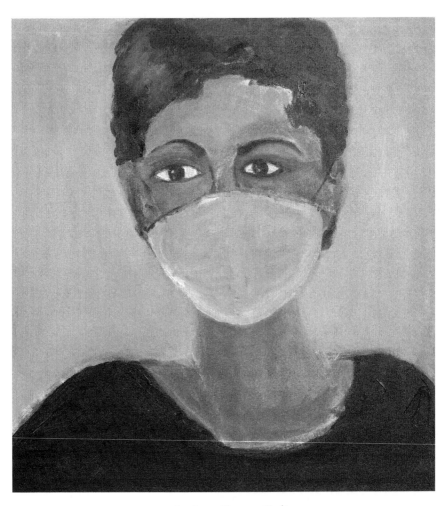

−painting, Karen Zelin

Time Out

To hear the birds singing their melodious songs...

To inhale the fragrance of flowers and trees on an early morning walk...

To observe the beauty of the flowers, and

To really examine the colors and exquisite petal designs...

To spend time savoring the sweet flavor of just-ripened fruit...

To recognize the organic beauty so often overlooked...

To notice the creativity and stepping up of people's kindness...

The daily appreciations of being in Time Out.

Sally Jones
"an elder's perspective"
June 2020

Everything Changes, Everything Ends

Life for many has changed dramatically this year with lost jobs, illness, and isolation. I am one of the lucky ones, yet even I struggle with how my daily routine has changed.

This is one of those times when I remind myself of the Buddhist teaching of impermanence. "Everything changes and everything ends." Change often catches me by surprise, but anticipating and accepting change helps me to cope with times like this.

I have experienced both joyful changes that set my heart aglow and devastating changes that left me grief stricken. This only reminds me that I need to value and nurture what I have and love now and to live in the present. All I have and love will change and end.

My body ages, my mind is not as sharp, fences fall down, possessions wear out, breakdown or are lost. Relationships progress or fade away. My temporarily-abled body will lose abilities. The stock market will fluctuate. Fog will eventually dissipate and the sun will return. My house that seems so stable and enduring will, in a thousand years, have been replaced, or may become an archeological site of past civilization; but still, I take care of it.

I walk through the forest and contemplate that all the plants and trees living today will eventually reach the end of their life cycles, hopefully to be replaced by others. But still, I treat them tenderly.

Every person currently alive on the planet as we speak will be dead in a little over 100 years, including all of us. We are part of the larger process of evolution, life unfolding in each moment. I look over the ocean to the horizon in amazement at the planet we inhabit—billions of years in the making of this moment in time. I imagine it may take billions more years before the planet either explodes into oblivion, or in much less time will simply be trashed beyond recognition. I hope this doesn't happen, and will work to keep it healthy, but even our planet will not last forever.

I am saddened over difficult changes both personal and universal. When I inevitably lose things and people I love, I grieve. Grief and mourning are gifts that have helped me to cope with loss. I also grieve for my country over changes manifested in this current reality show we are pulled into. However hard to accept, acceptance is the first step to creating the change we want. Some changes we do have some control over.

All this has me spending a lot of my time appreciating the things I do like and the people I love as they are now. When I accept that everything changes and everything ends, I experience life as precious. Life's fleeting moments are to be savored. When my time assuredly ends, I will have gotten the best of this brief time in the evolving process of which I am fortunate to be a part.

Mary Kay Hamilton

Global Rebound

The earth wobbles on her axis
and the wobble is increasing.
Humans are partly responsible
for the shaky rotations and revolutions
by causing climate change
which is causing the melting of glaciers
which is causing ocean levels to rise
which is impacting our wobble.
The wobble isn't a prelude to any
*environmental calamity**
which is a relief...
one global environmental calamity is enough.

People don't really worry
about the wobble though
because 1. they don't know about it
or 2. it's too abstract.
Why worry about something
you can't see or feel

like a virus.
I mean, it's not like
an earthquake
or a flood
or a tornado
or a tsunami.
I mean, you don't look
at a tornado approaching
your house and say
I think it's a hoax.

But then I think:
well, our lives are being
turned upside down
so maybe...we are feeling the wobble.

Earth does try to regain
her original shape,
glacial rebound it's called
and it's a slow process
very slow.

Maybe we humans
mimic our mother earth
trying to regain balance
as we walk on shaky ground
only ourselves to lean on.

Linda Serrato

*Trevor Nace, "Humans Are Causing Earth to Wobble
More as It Spins, NASA Finds," Forbes, 9.24.18*

Essential

I have been labeled an "essential worker." I do not think I like the term, but I do feel truly fortunate to have a job that can have a positive impact on peoples' lives. I am a registered nurse and have cared for patients with COVID-19. It has forever changed the way I do my job and allowed me to connect with patients in a new way.

These past few months have been surreal. The hospital I work in does not look the same. It does not operate the same. My coworkers look different. I feel changed. I have seen fear not only in the eyes of my patients, but also in the eyes of nurses and physicians. We take an oath to care for patients and often this means being exposed to infectious diseases. The uncertainty of this novel virus makes it feel different.

We even have a new term—"enhanced precautions"—requiring Personal Protective Equipment that includes a protective face shield (I purchased mine at a local welding supply company) in addition to an N95 mask, gown and gloves. The sequence of donning and doffing this equipment is of utmost importance and I find myself following the chart taped on the door every single time, even though I could do it in my sleep. It is that scary. I have had coworkers take a leave of absence rather than risk being exposed to the corona virus. The fears are not about the threat to us but rather about putting our loved ones in harm's way.

A couple of weeks into the shelter-in-place, I had a meltdown of sorts. I ran into Target to grab a couple of items and came out feeling deflated. How could people seemingly be acting as if life were "normal"? Families out shopping with kids in tow, no face masks, no social distancing. I got back to the car and surrendered to the tears. Earlier in the week I had heard the anguish in a woman's voice as she spoke to her dying mom via Zoom because she was not allowed to visit her in the hospital. I felt angry and betrayed that these people did not seem to get it.

Sadly, I find that still to be the case.

In my day-to-day interaction with patients, this pandemic has made me a better nurse. It has honed my senses to the patients' feelings. They are in the hospital for reasons that are scary; now add the threat of getting this virus in the mix. And they are alone. I think that is the hardest part. I held the hand of a woman my age as she was told her cancer had metastasized. She came in thinking she needed her gall-bladder removed and found out she had pancreatic cancer that had already spread to her liver. This is not the kind of news that anyone should hear alone. I stood next to her bed and became her family. I cried with her as she shared how close she was with her 18-year-old son and how she was not afraid of dying, only of leaving the ones she loved most to deal with the loss.

COVID-19 is still with us. The numbers of positive patients in our hospital have not gone down. We still only allow visitors on a limited basis. I am required to wear a face mask for the entire twelve-plus hours I am there, apart from my lunch break. I do not think that will change any time soon. Nurses have always had the task of advocating for their patients, but the connection I feel with my patients has taken on a deeper meaning now. That is my silver lining.

Lisa DeSocio-Sweeney, RN
June, 2020

From the Ashes

Up to this moment
    the songs of the morning starlings always brought hope.
Today their sounds seem a monotonous intrusion.
Past prayers of comfort
    seem they were meant for a different person.
And now a rumbling from deep inside
    heralds a darkness which threatens to swallow me whole.

The garden kale has gone to seed.
Unpicked tangerines lay bird pecked and rotting up in the tree.
Skies are blackened with smoke from tear gas and festering rage.
News of death and grim predictions cry out from every direction.

But I have turned enough pages in my life to know the story is ever
    changing.
There are always surprise plot twists
    and characters transformed by their own pain and reckless decisions.
In dire circumstances there can be miraculous survival.

Reaching out over the chasm of uncertainty we look to see who is there
    what we are holding in our hands extended out in blessing
    and what path lies beckoning.

New wisdom can emerge from need and despair.
Thresholds call for courage, yours and mine together.
And here we are, indomitable and relentless.
The cheerful optimists who know about darkness before dawn.
The change makers fiercely determined to use the current momentum
    to enact new legislation.
The artists, musicians and poets who are rising on every abandoned
    lot and street corner.
The scientists, steadily pulsing knowledge, steadfast in the belief
    that the truth will set us free.
And in my garden
    the bright daffodils peek through the weeds of my neglect and
    complacency
    urging me to wake up.

The chaos and the beauty all around are reflections of who we are.
It is a time of the Great Fire and we are being called to rise.
But it is not just my small self lifting from these ashes.
WE are the phoenix, one pulsing body of flapping wings and flashing
    sunlight.

I start again always from the beginning.
Walking to the ocean's edge
I splash water on my face in a baptism of hope.
Turning to the mountains I lean in to listen.
Redwoods offer their silent wisdom,
    Stay steady. Stay strong. Stay connected.
    Keep reaching for the light.

Sarojani Rohan

First Day, Social Distancing–photo, Sara Friedlander

Hidden Blessings

As we shelter in place,
nature regenerates eroded ozone.
Deer and mountain lions reclaim community parks.
Highways are empty,
Sushi Heaven shuttered.

Quarantine gives us space
for meditation, reconnecting with earth.
The Pacific soothes, sluices ashore,
sprinkles the beach with broken sand dollars,
feathers, frayed sections of rope.
Ocean waves reshape granite headlands,
smooth jagged rock into polished moonstones.

In the bay, whales spout and breach,
shelter their calves before heading south.
Over Fisherman's Wharf,
blackbirds tango with seagulls.
Tides rise and fall.
Daylight cycles into darkness.
Sunrise returns.

Jennifer Lagier

hope, now, is harder to find in strangers' faces

but my seventy-year old neighbor leaves letters on my
    doorstep, thanking me for the poetry books i lend to her
        and confides in me the days after her husband died last
            august how he had half a foot and half a leg amputated.

hope, now, is harder to find in strangers' faces
    but it's become easier to fall in love with peoples'
        eyes to remember where they crease above a
        hidden smile
            i am thankful that life and love will never be the same again.

when i bump elbows in the store i
    shudder in paranoid fear.
        but there is also an excitement.
            that despite this isolation,
                my body is still (t)here, able to be felt,
                    able to be touched in tender mistake.
                        and god, what a thrill.

Clem Peterson

What to Do During a Major Environmental Catastrophe
(Deepwater Horizon, 2010)

Cook dinner.
Love your spouse.
Check the news. It's bad.
Cook dinner again. Obsessively read about "top kill,"
the latest plan, mud, old tires and everything
being shoved into our earth's belly
to stop the dark hemorrhaging.
Pray it works.
Pray.
Cook dinner again.
It's failed.
Weep a full morning.
Love your spouse.
Stare at the sky. Stop reading the news.
Check the news: No End In Sight.
Contemplate the end of the world.
Or the end of all you've known.
Feel alarm settle into your bones.
It will not leave this summer.
Cook dinner again. Clean the countertops.
Scrub the kitchen floor.
Wake in the middle of the night
to write in your notebook.
Hurricanes are coming.
It's raining in your heart.
The seas have turned black.
It is absolutely impossible to live.
Cook dinner.

Carolyn Flynn

Spin the Human
2010

Blindfolded, I am at the center of a circle drawn in colored chalk on the driveway called Spin the Human. There are many points along the wheel, each naming an event gleaned from current events. As I spin, I wonder . . . which one will it be?

1. Opening the hunting ground for international killing of great whales
2. 50,000 gallons of oil spewing into the Gulf of Mexico with no end in sight
3. Kindergarteners, 29 stabbed in China
4. Wars in Iraq and Afghanistan
5. Climate change, worldwide refugees
6. Poverty, hunger, homelessness

I find joy with the grandchildren. We play in the park, read stories, make May baskets, while a subtitle runs beneath the surface: what will be here for these children in their lifetime? We read about how beavers, seals and birds make their homes. Will animals still be here? Why must our grandsons learn they are at risk by wearing red or blue in the wrong place at the wrong time? Are we doing these children a disservice? Will the shock of what's left by the time they're fifteen or twenty create a disillusionment too deep and distressing to manage?

"Look—a roly poly!" Rumi, three, squeals, transfixed by a little bug. Amir, five, climbs a pepper tree, Superman ready to fly. Holding back tears, I want to protect them, stop the march of destruction . . . because there's nowhere to run!

If only—if only we could somehow, collectively, wake up from our illusions.

I draw a new circle with possibilities. Blindfolded, I spin. Round and round I go.

I land on The Here and Now: the See-able, the Do-able.

"Come together, right now!"

Break bread and sing!

Judy Phillips

–photo, Kate Aver Avraham, Capitola CA

Home

What has happened to my normal?
My going about, getting my hair done,
shopping, making plans to go out for dinner,
having family parties and weekend guests.
It's all different now.
There has been an unexpected and
frightening upheaval at the source of life
as I knew it.

Crazy to say but I feel released.
I am free floating and realize I don't want to
go back to my habits and rhythms before the
weight of this pandemic has kept us sheltered at home.
I thought I was awake but I wasn't because
I was surrounded by the ease of everyday
entitled expectations.

We just bought a house. We were longing
for a home and this sweet gift presented itself
in the midst of this tectonic shift.
This is what my heart is seeking. As I was
meditating today my mind wandered to the new
garden we will create and the babies who will
come to play on blankets under the shade tree.

In the yard, tangerines are ripe and dropping.
Delicious gifts ready to eat. Meyer lemons are
ready to be picked outside the front door. The
front porch beckons. A wee dram of whiskey, sitting
in the gloaming as the light softly dims and the sky darkens.

There will be fairy lights in the trees, urns filled
with flowers and a fountain inviting peace.
We will grow herbs and tomatoes and whatever else
takes our fancy. As I write this I am seeing clearly
what is next. This urge to create a new nest is so powerful.
To feel grounded. A real home at last.

I am seeking a more contemplative life, a more
grateful life. I am in love with the earth and I crave deeper
roots so that I can show my gratitude to her.
The word resilience keeps coming up too. Going with the flow
of dynamic change wherever it leads me. Eyes open, keeping the
mantra of change alive in meditation every day. Stay in the game!
Stay in the mix! Keep the power of the Goddess moving me forward.

Anne Stafford-Wade

Phoenix

In these hollow days of isolation,
I live in a wilderness
of redwood trees, raptors, tiny feeding birds,
peacefulness as motionless
as a great horned owl at midnight.

Chaos shudders everywhere else.
Contagion binds us all
to the reminder that nothing is forever.

Even Mother Earth shrugs
her resigned shoulders, tired
of begging us to intervene.

Outside my window, reluctant sun
plays coy with persistent gray gloom.
I find the knife-sharp edge of grief
for every living thing cutting me
while I wait for emergent light.

Suddenly, a red-shouldered hawk
lands on the fence outside,
swivels his commanding head until
his piercing gaze finds me, locks on . . .

I am drawn into a wisdom
far beyond my fragile aging self,
tired aching bones.

We have been scoured, scraped raw
to the core of what we've been
and may or may not be.

What we laid aside to make it through
falls short as paychecks, investments, dreams,
relationships collapse.
We are left looking at each other
naked and as real as when we were born.

Take up that infant of what is true,
cradle it close to your beating heart . . .
even Phoenix, burned to ashes,
rose again, renewed.

Kate Aver Avraham

Simplicity

Hope and resilience blossom from seeds of love and kindness. When strangers organize food drives, or a professional researcher takes a job as a cleaning woman in a nursing home to visit her quarantined husband, or a family clears debris from a disabled man's yard, or a senior citizen donates his stimulus check to a food bank—such flowering of genuine humanity keeps me optimistic. Generosity of the human spirit and expressions of human goodness remind me that even when times seem dark, light also lives in the shadows. By paying closer attention to "good" news and minimizing consumption of depressing news, I keep my oars rowing toward strength instead of helplessness.

Here in Santa Cruz with the Pacific Ocean, long stretches of beach, redwood forests, mountains and healthy air, nature's canvas is vibrant and giving. I do my best to get in hikes and walks where reality consists mostly of the sounds of bird, wind and waves and the sights of tall trees, leafy greenery or lush blue-green water. While inhaling the beauty of the natural world I am transported from worries into magnificence.

For quiet reflection, I engage in daily sitting meditation. This stillness can be accessed regardless of what may be troubling in the rest of the world. When worries arise, I lean on the memory of these calmer states to ease me gently into whatever I might need to confront. Prayer provides another available pathway towards a positive way forward. It becomes a catalyst for transforming discomfort and doubts into open space for letting go and new possibilities.

Sometimes as my thoughts churn and challenges whirl, I discover droplets of poetry and prose bubbling up and my words pour out on paper. I write. Writing becomes a form of medicine that relieves ruminations and concerns. Others' writing also inspires and I soak in their brilliance. Especially now, in these turbulent times of fear and insecurity, I seek out novels by authors of diverse cultures, countries and backgrounds offering their own heartaches and solutions, and expose myself to their perspectives. My empathy muscles expand as I connect through stories of the oneness of the human family.

While zoom technology doesn't replace close-up intimacy, it offers the ability to be in emotional and visual proximity and has become an indispensable resource for which I am grateful. As the landscape of our world changed so abruptly, many familiar comforts needed to be reimagined. The exhilaration enjoyed from in-person gatherings, shared meals and celebrations has fizzled, yet the healing essences of these events—love and belonging—can still thrive. I use zoom to keep in contact with meetings, meaningful activities and classes so that my social network remains somewhat whole. In these difficult times, I look for ways to keep healthy supports in place, though the form may change.

In my own family, about a dozen relatives from ages 20 through 90 look forward to zoom each week with a preselected theme. We've shared favorite movies, books, songs, photos, jokes, dreams, flowers, trees and even superpowers. We live in Hawaii, New York, North Carolina, Arizona and California, and rarely were able to come together. Now we take advantage of time at home to convene regularly in new, fun and deeper ways. This renewed sense of belonging helps wash away isolation and distance.

Though it may be obvious, I need to mention friendship. Without those listening ears and knowing wisdom of friends, I would feel much less grounded. Many of my walks are with earbuds attached to my phone and a friend on the other end of the line, blending exercise and companionship. For those friends nearby, we take socially distanced walks and visits and normalize our routines as much as feasible.

Last, I draw strength from knowledge. Whether confronting COVID, politics, racism, immigration, relationships, illness, or death and dying, I seek information to stand on my own feet and move with integrity. I learn to discover common ground amidst diverse viewpoints, and seek ways my gifts and skills can be of service.

Highlighting the good builds hope. When I notice love emanating in any of its multitudinous shapes, healing, resilience and renewal all spread their enormous and exquisite wings like birds in flight.

Ratna Jennifer Sturz

Prayer Flags

learning to open
doors with an elbow
coronavirus

sheltering in place—
cherry trees bloom
in an empty park

at midnight
I almost hear them
frogs singing

soaking the reed
of her college clarinet
quarantine

kelp wrack
wishing she could walk
on water

how little
gets done in a day
floating seed puffs

the taste
of a wild blackberry
summer drizzle

neighborhood walk
the stick that looks like a snake
hasn't moved

what we take
and what we leave behind
honey harvest

sneaking a cherry
under her mask
checkout line

reading poetry
to the delphinium
August moon

hugging
the tree tighter
autumn loneliness

still home
sourdough starter handed
over the fence

Dyana Basist

In the world of haiku, there is a quiet tradition called a ginko walk. Either a solo person or a group of haiku poets amble along alertly, often in nature, just noting, then jotting down "what is": the gleam of a leaf, a raven's wing tilting, a child giggling from behind a fence . . .

During this pandemic I have continued wandering with my small notebook. The practice of the one-breath haiku has acted like a darning needle, mending my days together into weeks, now months. A haiku birthing is one of beauty but also surprise. Simple but not easy. I bow to its ancient Japanese roots and ever-evolving form. -DB

−photo, Lauren Crux

Get Carried Away

Carry away my wife, my dog,
my house, my life. Remove
from me every memory.

Let me drift free and uneasy,
an anchorless ship, cloud
bearing north by northwest—

wait, it's shifting east. Free me
from this body. Mount me
on a kite, let me soar over

enemy lines at a height beyond
all arrows. Let me report on what
I spy on the other side

of reality when I'm no longer alive
except as the trees and rocks are,
those quieter speakers saying

what is is all in the present tense,
tensionless, pure being, instead
of this labored breathing.

David Sullivan

The Thread

I first learned to meditate when I was fifteen years old, when Mahatma Fakiranand, a *mahatma* of young Guru Maharaj ji, selected me for a Knowledge session in the basement of the *premie* house in Bayonne, New Jersey. I was the youngest in the room, chosen for my youth and supposed purity, even though I'd only heard *satsang*, the company of truth, once—the night before. I'd cut school and hitchhiked to the address, wadded up on a piece of paper shoved in my jeans pocket, and then from the train station to the dark basement with the orange shag carpet and a huge picture of Guru Maharaj ji in a gilt-edged frame, set on white silk on an ornate wooden carved chair.

"Would you cut your head off for Guru Maharaj ji?" was the question Mahtama-ji asked me.

"Yes," I said, prostrating on the floor, as my mouth tickled by the synthetic threads of the shag rug. "Yes, I would."

Ten minutes later, he touched my third eye and initiated me. He taught me about the divine music, the divine light, the sacred, holy nectar and the sacred Word of God, found in the space between breaths—that quiet, silent holy *Ahhhhh....*

For the first time, I was instructed to follow my breath. To track the inhale, the exhale, the space before, the space afterwards. The space in between. I moved into the ashram as a teenager, but I was a crappy meditator. I've always been a crappy meditator. I love my mind too much. Maybe.

But I've never forgotten my breath. It was there when I took too much acid on a mountain top with my father at 23; when I felt I was being ripped to pieces, my breath was the boat I rode home. When I was in labor, Eliza barreling through my body in two short hours like a runaway freight train, my breath brought her into the world.

When the doors closed and the mask came over my face the morning of my cancer surgery, my breasts covered with magic marker words from my children: "Take care of my mom." "This one," Eli had instructed in bold black letters on my right breast. "Not this one," he'd written on the left one.

As that mask came over my face and I started to drift, I remembered my breath. As I have every time I have come up short, every time I've been awash in rage or dread or panic or fear, when I have not known what to do or how to cope, when incest memories assailed me, when my mother screamed at me when I came out to her, "You've confirmed my worst fear about you," I have always returned to my breath.

When my father lay dying, I told the team to back off and not resuscitate him, breathed as I watched him take his last breath. Inhale, exhale. And the space in between. When my mother lay dying, I aligned my breath with hers.

And now we are in a time of pandemic. Every morning, I sit on the purple fainting couch in our living room or straight up in bed, put on my headphones and listen to another calm, sonorous voice telling me to tend to my breath. To notice. To slide my attention up and down. To feel each micromovement of life moving through my belly, my chest, my esophagus.

It doesn't matter that I suck at it. It only matters that I do it. It only matters that I know that between the moment of my birth, when my identical twin Vicki was left behind, when I was catapulted into the world alone, the lights an assault on my frail tiny premie body, there was breath, and that breath will stay with me until the moment of my death—whether it is from old age or cancer or on a ventilator with COVID-19. Whether my loved ones are there or I am alone—and let's face it, we *always* die alone—my breath will be there until it isn't. Until the very last one.

The amazing life force that is my personality rides on my breath like a tight wire. All that doing. All that giving. All that force of nature that is my life, riding on my breath. The same breath you are breathing now. The same breath the Senators are breathing. The House members who are not in session. All the politicians. The ones who opened their states too early. The ones who didn't. My steady hero: Gavin Newsom. My haircutter who cannot work. My son, Eli, and his fiancé, Jenny, who had COVID-19—who now are well. And our daughter, Eliza, flying kites on the roof in Amman with her boyfriend, Essam, on the weekends when it is illegal to leave their apartment under risk of arrest. All the people in Amman are flying kites and pigeons and the call to prayer still rises up through the empty streets. They are all breathing.

And it's not just people I love. The ones I respect and admire. It's everyone. The people protesting in the capitals demanding to open their tanning salons because of their pride at being able to support their families, suddenly taken away. Those who want things to stay shut down. Those who want them to open. Those who want to shelter in place. Those who believe in science. Those who follow the tweets of a madman. The fools who actually went ahead and drank bleach. Those who believe we're overreacting—that the virus is a plot, a campaign trip, a hoax. My friend who says she won't leave her home for two years or longer—until there is a vaccine.

Those terrified of dying. Those who want life back the way it was—who are only asking for self-determination. Those who insist their right to work matters more than the numbers of dead no one can agree on. Those who will survive this epidemic and those who won't—all of us, every single human being on the planet, all of us vibrating our life force within this pandemic, all of us breathing. All living beings. Breathing.

The plants and animals and fish and birds and dolphins breathing in cleaner air. All of us hoping this will be the great reckoning that brings in a golden age of justice and ecological balance and racial equality and respect for life. And those who want to grab more. Pillage the earth more.

Every single one of us—breathing. All of us in this dance of life and death. Dependent on that inhale and exhale. None of us knowing—not really—what tomorrow will bring. All of us so confused because how can we know the future when we live in a world dripping with misinformation, disinformation, endless righteous sources of information. No one knows. Our future is unknowable.

There is only the now. This whole pandemic is a giant crash course in the now. This breath. This body. This moment. This inhale. This exhale. That thread that carries us from the beginning to the end. We are one body breathing. Breathing in the ultimate uncertainty. And there is no way to escape it.

Laura Davis

Pandemic Paradox
Two Poems in Plague Time

1

On my morning walk,
a young couple
in shorts and tee shirts
advertising the local gym
run abreast as they
blindly eye each other.

Blocking the sidewalk,
they force me to veer
into traffic to avoid them.

I vow in the future
to wear a tee shirt
that says . . .

"Don't sneeze or cough on me!"
on a field of Corona viruses
emblazoned on the front
and "Six feet apart
or six feet under!"
on the back.

2

Six feet apart,
we are more
aware than ever
six degrees of separation
are all that divide us.

Dan Phillips

The Sacred Pause

I come from a long line of worriers.
Early in the pandemic I went through a litany of fears and paranoias.
I worried I might inhale an offending airborne droplet.
That I wasn't washing my hands well enough.
Or sanitizing my cell phone, my steering wheel, my doorknobs.
That I might open the mail too soon before decontaminating.

I worried that the food supply might run out.
Or electricity could sputter to a halt.
That our health care system could collapse.
That anarchy would dominate the streets.
And desperate people will do desperate things.
I harbor no illusions. These are current realities for many,
and could become so for me and my community.

But I have decided to release myself from these fears.
If these are the end times, or my end time,
or the end of life as we've known it—
I want to be fully present.
I want to find all the joy that I can.
Walk barefoot on the damp grass. Explore new trails.
Revel in the profusion of spring flowers—
the way orange plays with purple and green.
Make the matzoh ball soup, the apple crisp.
Dance in the living room on a Tuesday afternoon.
Reach out to a friend. Find ways to laugh.
I will not be taken down by angst—mine or anyone else's.

My ancestors wrestled with trauma.
They escaped pogroms, traveled a vast ocean,
learned new language and culture,
saved money and resources so their children would thrive
and be free from oppression.
I'm not about to knuckle under now.

I've planted sunflowers and zinnias, bok choy and collards.
I live among farmers and farmland. I will not fear hunger and starvation.
I donate to food banks as I bow and kiss the earth
in gratitude for my abundance.

I pay attention to the news, but don't dwell on it.
Like the five blind men describing the elephant—
there are many versions and perspectives.
So much spin. Science is challenged. Conspiracy theories abound.
I won't allow my head and heart to be highjacked by one leg of the elephant.

I send loving kindness to my fellow beings. So much suffering.
So much unknown.
We are being called to something deep and profound.
The sacred pause is revealing our fault lines. Our misguided thinking.
Our urgent need for transformation. For prioritizing Life.
Emerging stronger, wiser, kinder.

Along the way, on this rocky road—I find I am changing.
I am somehow, miraculously, finally, trusting.

Marigold Fine
August 3, 2020

Apricot Pie

Maybe I will make an apricot pie
Cook those apricots until their sweetness
Arrives at its peak
To grace our taste buds with their orange glory

Oh yes I have felt glory during this odd, odd time
When I made the peach pie, I ate most all of it myself
Just last month   my birthday month   the month of June

I promised my friends to give them a piece, but
I failed to fulfill that promise,
Only full-filling my own stomach instead
It just goes to show what an odd odd time this is

If I promise, it's a done deal. I always follow through

Now I want to be able to knock on their doors,
Carrying a nice quarter of peach pie filled with deliciousness
        sit down at their tables and watch their
Eyes widen and their mouths smile
As they eat and we share tea, and talk face to face.

But now it is facemask to facemask and that's odd
But okay
Okay because it has to be
The easy knock on one another's door is gone for now
And in its place is the heart

The heart of the matter
What is the matter now is the threat of getting sick, really sick
For our age
The mid-sixties and early seventies our age bracket

We have to have brackets around us now
Everyone has to have brackets–
      face masks cover our smiles
We elders have to be more careful
Washing our hands until our thinner skin chaps a bit

It's true that we have developed thick skin over our years
Thick skin that sees
This will pass, sometime
too long is . . . sometime

Endurance is the key

Endurance of day to day hour to hour minute to minute
the breath to breathe in and out
As we near this race's finish line

Jean Mahoney

Early Pandemic

The smoky dim grayness of fog veils a single shaft of sunlight passing through the willowy trees outside my bedroom window . . . Faintly, a single bird chirps its dawn song through the open passageway of my garden door . . . a space now vacant of the whooshing sounds of the early morning cars carrying the workforce north and south on the roads above.

A hush has fallen on the Earth, quieting what is called the world. A Canopy of Clarity, pure fresh atmosphere—the bluest sky seen in decades reveals itself, as clouds of human activity below slowly stall, and stop, and rest in place.

A gloom has descended into the hearts of humans, as a corona encircles the planet, with a reckoning force and no goal short of a takeover.

Yet Peace is present in every empty street and townhall, knocking on doors; unmasked, she offers a warm handshake into the silent shelters of our hearts.

Slowly a Call to Love is rising up, whispering like women sharing secrets, entering the dry hollows of our ears . . . "Return, return," it sings, "it's true, it's true."

We were born for a time like this . . .

Donna Runnalls

Hope (Lockdown Lifted)–Mixed Media, Bob Nielsen

What have we done?

We rob the soil of our own decaying bodies
locked in impenetrable lead

We empty the earth-bowels of its oils
burn them into the poison we breathe

We enslave trees into rows of unnatural sameness
resembling the drone of our own disconnect

The animals who generously fed us for millennia
we degrade into insane bio-machines
and then ingest their pain

We vomit insoluble debris into the waters
then bottle what's drinkable for profit

Please, as you behold Corona
save your surprise for other stars
We have poked into the mystery
with the wrong finger one too many times
the answer is here

And now listen

May the grief and the fear
may the loss and the changes
compost into wisdom
beyond the creative responses
that illuminate our days of reclusion
with the value of connection and pause

May this creativity be more than
a resourceful distraction to overcome the discomfort of now
and generate new words for love

May it turn into a NO
to unchecked greed and exploitation
No to injustice and pollution
to senselessly consuming the life force that feeds us
No to blindness, deafness, discrimination
No
a NO for every day nested in the domesticity of small choices

May a choir of yes to sanity resonate through the planet
building a critical mass of right action
right thought
right relationship
right pauses
right silence
right taking
right giving
right waiting
right for all organic siblings and inorganic kin
right to live in natural wealth guided by dreams
right for the little people
and their old brown gods of roots and seeds
willing, at last, to try peace

Mariabruna Sirabella
3/30/2020

She Who Questions–Mariabruna Sirabella

I do not welcome this chaos, but I am not surprised of finding myself in its midst. I turn to what has always nourished me, my great teacher: nature. Possibly more urgently than ever, She urges me to listen, look, relate, reflect, and change. She Responds. She Questions. I create all alone like when I was a kid, sitting on the floor. I metabolize in my Soul-Collage® cards the pleasure of the slower pace and the creative challenges along with grief, losses, and injustice. -MS

Chrysalis

I close my eyes and I am a wide winged ancient bird swooping
over the forests of our earth.
I dip low, skimming the treetops breathing deeply, drunk on oxygen.
Knowing I am safe above the canopy I land, swaying on a skinny branch,
looking past the neverending green to the bright blue sea
at the end of the world.

When I open my eyes my vision is blurred by tears of loss.
I feel the heart pain of great suffering all around me.
Yet, there is great courage, creativity and the joining.
The mantra "we are all in this together" gives me hope that we will
survive this catastrophe.

I see and know that we are in a Chrysalis of Sequester. Forming, becoming
and readying to emerge not knowing what we will find.
We will be newborns full of love, compassion and strength
ushering in the deep change that comes with the awakening of
perfect beating hearts on fire.

Anne Stafford-Wade

Offerings

There is a heartache in the land.
It sits behind closed doors, in silent rooms.
It sits in mother's hearts and upon the lover's shoulder.
It hovers at the crest of a wave
and moves past us on empty streets.
We are suddenly alone.

What is our recourse, our salvation?
It is not "to take arms against a sea of troubles
and by opposing, end them."
It is not by might that we will vanquish this foe,
but with gentleness and grace.

It is to know that the despair we find in ourselves
belongs to us all. It is but one piece of who we are,
one chapter in the sojourn of our lives.

We can hold high ground for one another.
I am here to let you fall and pick you up again.
And when I raise my eyes from the muddy creek,
I'll look up and see you waiting on the path.

Together we will walk ahead,
presenting our offerings as we always have.
We will walk and talk and laugh and love.
We will take to the streets for justice
and for peace.
We will learn new ways,
cover our faces and stand further
from one another than we like.

Mingling along the ether
we will take to the airwaves of our minds.
We will write and paint and beat the drum.
We will bake and clean and romp
and hike and bike and dance.
We will embrace the shelter that we create
and remain our human selves.

Like children we seesaw up and down,
dependent on one another for balance
and for grace.

Nina Koocher

Walk Among the Living

Even if I'm drunk on loss
wishing some amnesia
would take me
to the tabula rasa
of a new day
where yesterday's voice
can't recite the same old story
in my Ferris wheel mind
of the singular moment
that slammed the brakes
on my dreams —

I face the mirror
exhale the past
look with love
upon the creature
I am
and continue to walk
among the living.

Maggie Paul
from Scrimshaw
Hummingbird Press

–drawing, Enid Baxter Ryce

We Couldn't Have Done It Without Us–painting, Sarah Bianco

The ARGUMENT for LOVE

–painting, Sonia Calderón

After Machado

Out of the broken branch
the child makes a broom.

Out of cracked clay pots
a mosaic forms.

In the unwhole hearts
of all creatures,
the argument for love.

Maggie Paul
from Borrowed World
Hummingbird Press

I Came into the World

My father was there, my mother.
I came into a room where the table was laid
as if for a banquet, figs on white plates,
cool water. Like a stranger, I stood aside, hesitant.
Music rose up and pushed against the ceiling,
shimmered there like a crystal chandelier.
People were singing. The floor shook with dance.
I came into a house where I was a stranger
and was made welcome.
My mother gave me her body, my father
his voice. I stood between them, faltering.
The walls of the house rose up around us.
The roof shuddered with the sound of wind and rain.
Birds settled in the rafters. At night we could hear them,
the shuffling of feathers, melodies marking territory,
saying, *This is mine; this is real.*

Gail Newman
from Blood Memory
Marsh Hawk Press, 2020

Laundry, 1952

My mother is hanging laundry on the line.
As usual, it's summer in my memory,
the light tender and trembling.
She snaps wooden clothespins onto cotton slips,
shirts, white socks, balancing the pins in her mouth.
From the upstairs window, I watch her move
around the yard in a flowered house dress
that ties in back like an apron.
Behind her the insect drone of freeway traffic,
and beyond the alley heading west
lies the ocean, white shoulders
of sand, palm trees and the green horizon.
As she works, stringing up long sheets and pillowcases,
she lifts her arms and looks toward the window
where I watch, but she can't see me as I pull back
behind the venetian blinds. I can see the part in her hair,
her pale calves and low-heeled shoes,
eyes squinting through thick glasses.
All year I have been watching her like this,
a voyeur looking out of a window
as if there were something in that body
I could, for a short time, borrow or store away
as reference for a later date.

Gail Newman
from Blood Memory
Marsh Hawk Press, 2020

ᜋᜆᜓᜃ ᜋ ᜐ ᜶ ᜊᜒᜋ᜔ᜄᜓᜊᜋ

i awoke where sky met water
langit opened and *tubig* flowed through

so my mother called me *ilog diwata*, river spirit, or that-which-runs-into-the-ocean

when i was four i wouldn't speak, so my grandmother brought me to the dakit tree
let me climb its hanging roots. she said *dalhín mo ang pag-kakataóng* called me *babaylan*, that-which-from-the-ocean-arises

and i realized the tree was cradling me, *dala mula bathalá*
to a place without words or witness, *salita saksí laho*
where i became water
my hands ripples
dila katha

that-which-carries-us-home

Cassidy Parong

My poems are pieces of regeneration: my strength is drawn from my mother, and her mother before—and down the line (I like to imagine) all the way into the first womb, the Primordial Womb, where the flesh extends into lava, and the sinews salt and ash. From this earth belly I draw these poems. –CP

−photo, Lauren Crux

−photo, Nina Koocher, Arles France

Becoming a Father

We circle as a tribe
father, son, brother, and friends
grass, trees, sun and wind
along with the echoes of our ancestors
who whisper their wisdom tenderly and with zeal.
They stand with staff and plow; the prophet and the wizard.
Inviting you, a new father, to make your way into the forest
where no path has yet been groomed nor cleared
and the way to proceed is with the heart
for a map is too fixed and unclear.
Though you are not alone in this domestic venture.
First, you have your own breath
to remind you of who you are;
father, son, brother and friend.
You have your family who will help bind this trail
through the thicket and over the pass.
And you have this moment encompassed
with those who have come before you
and those who stand now beside you.
We are here as reminders, you are enough.
And we are all children growing up.

Bill Underwood
2020

The Journey

My father does not come
to me in dreams, though I wait,
patient as a monk, bags packed
to join him on his journey.

He is so deeply asleep that even the angels
cannot wake him, though they might blow
onto his face, fly with wings spread like sieves
for the light of the world to pass through,
pluck at his body, worrying his soul.

I will never see my father again.
Still, sometimes I feel him beside me,
sharpening tools, salting potatoes, breathing.

When I open my mouth his words fly out,
when I open my eyes, his tears.

Gail Newman
from Blood Memory
Marsh Hawk Press, 2020

Journeyman

Remember the time when I went
To work with you every day.
You were an early riser.
Not me! Poor you!
You had to wake me.

You made me porridge and tea.
I watched you make sandwiches
And pack our lunches.
I had a Roy Rogers lunchbox.
You carried a black lunch bucket with
A big thermos of tea.
Sometimes my small thermos would
Be filled with chocolate milk.
You would drop me off at school.

After school I would walk down to
The house you were building.
I would sit on a sawhorse table and
Chatter on. You were a great audience
Laughing at my stories while you sawed
And nailed and hung perfect, beautiful
Cabinets.

You loved wood. You would show me
Special pieces you saved. I think
Mahogany was your favorite. I
Still have the toolbox you made and
All the beautiful tools you used every day.
You were a brilliant artisan. I don't think you
Saw yourself that way, but I did.

You had a farmer's tan and smelled of fresh
Sawdust when you hugged me.
Still my favorite fragrance, it makes me think
Of everything you meant to me.

Anne Stafford-Wade

The Vessel–painting, Sarah Bianco

The Lean Years

There were times back then
payday a week away,
I'd stand at the open fridge,
gather what was left:
lone carrot from the crisper,
a few stalks of celery,
the carton's last egg,
a heel of bread, and
from the cupboard,
a pack of soup mix,
handful of noodles,
some raisins in a bag,
last bit of flour from the bin.

And I'd conjure a meal
with the promise to fill,
forging from lack as
women know to do,
so that when I called you
from your fields of play,
your eyes lit with delight
at the food on the table.
And so you need not know
the want, I'd put a dab
on my plate too, say
I was full, sampled
too much while cooking.
And there, as you filled your belly,
recounted stories of your day,
all that I hungered for
in those spare years
was sated.

Gail Brenner

New Grandson

I walk outside, there we are now
Breath pulse and heart

I hold you in the cradle of my arms
There we are now
Breath pulse and heart

Brain not needed here
Only the 5,000 senses that
Say safety sweetness and wisdom

I walk outside, there we are now
Breath pulse and heart

I hold you in the cradle of my arms
There we are now
Breath
  pulse
    and heart

Jean Mahoney

Wee Dean–photo, Jean Mahoney

Pandemic Time Wisdom
from Joshua and Charlie, aka Pa

Joshua and Charlie live with their parents, Jane and Rich, and their two older brothers, Will and Austin. Jane is by heart a singer, and by profession directs and teaches in a private music school for kids. Rich is the pastor of a Presbyterian church. During these many weeks of global pandemic, the parents work from home and the family ventures out only of necessity and for short daily runs on the sidewalks that wind through the flat plain of their Los Angeles neighborhood. These runs are mainly for the sake of the parents as a way to run down the abundant energy of these robust little men, who anyway run back and forth over the house floors day and night.

For a family of six, the dwelling that holds them is small; three petite bedrooms and one bathroom serve the personal needs of six people, with an adjoining living and dining room and a one-way in-and-out kitchen. When I visit the family (and it's not too beastly hot) I utilize the family garage for my quarters, a space which houses a comfy sleeping sofa and three walls of floor to ceiling stacked and labeled boxes along with various camping and athletic equipment, games, and many Legos in drawers for the littler hands and imaginations to mold into greater worlds and creatures. Just outside the living room patio door is, thankfully, a relatively large expanse of green commonly known as the backyard.

During a recent visit after months of keeping distance, I was witness to a "transformational utilization project" in this family greenspace. The yard had sprouted a makeshift wooden clubhouse (designed, nailed and hammered by Dad), complete with windows and a small door, yielding entrance only to older folk who could still bend down far enough and curl up small enough to slide in. Aside the usual large containers of balls and swords and trucks was a new box containing an assortment of superhero costumes, including a few skirts and a couple of flowing scarves. Other new additions included a large green enameled bird feeder and a red hummingbird feeder. In the corner lay a large deflated swimming pool, a roll of plastic which revealed itself as a Slip N Slide, and a few small parked bikes and trucks.

Beyond this large peripheral array of civilized toys, the grassy rectangle stretches out to rows of tall shrubs and various flowing hibiscus and glossy camellia bushes in front of a perimeter fence, part of which is made of bamboo lacing, allowing a shadowy view of the neighbors' large dog, his curious nose outcropping between the bamboo poles. It is here I was to meet and greet the wildness and indomitable spirits of the two more recent arrivals to the family and Planet Earth, Joshua and Charlie.

Here, on most mornings, the day starts in costume. Five-year-old Joshua, bold and outspoken and also an intuitive and sensitive boy, leads the way for the pack of two brothers. Most days, his Superman is met by a strong-willed and angel-faced Charlie in his hand-me-down Batman suit. Charlie, at two-and-a-half, being presently of very few but very strong words, appears one day in a different guise. In one of the family's favorite rerun series, Little House on the Prairie, Michael Landon as Pa is almost always seen wearing a brown cowboy hat. Charlie, now in an oversized brown cowboy hat and boots, refuses to answer my address as Charlie. Instead, he states, "NO, no—NOT Charlie. I am PA, Call me PA!"

As the summer sun travels headlong over the yard, the layers of costumes and imagination melt away with the heat, and finally even the small underpants are tossed and two naked little men roam the green Earth in full glory. Due to the unimaginable supply of water allotted to southern California by the powers that be, the garden hose is often at work on these hot afternoons. Under the shade of generous trees, the boys and I occupy ourselves by digging for earthworms and relocating them temporarily to an earthworm home in a large glass container. As the worms are scarce and the ground tough, there is a lot of slow and careful digging with small sticks, much deep talk about the life of bugs, and time with the greatness of mud.

Yes, the mud! In one sloping corner of the yard dangles a rope tied high in the limb of the tree. During these afternoons, the territory under the rope becomes a small muddy lake with at least one small Tarzan climbing trees and swinging above it. Below, the two companions, Charlie and Grandma Amma, wade in the cool of water and shade and shout of bravery to the one above us.

On Sunday the family van makes its way to the presently empty church, and Dad in his ministerial duties is filmed and transmitted locally, with Jane and one other male choir member acting as a mini choir. During my stay, the little boys and I await the close of service in the official playroom with semi-gloss blue walls and overhead florescent lights, where the plastic toys are subject to any form of imagination that makes time pass more quickly. Upon returning home on this Sunday, the children are restless to eat lunch and return to the outside. Under my watch, their parents have the happy opportunity to go on a drive away from home (the first time alone together in three months). I remark to Joshua and Charlie that soon we three can venture out and play in the mud. Adamantly, Joshua states, "Amma—let me tell you how to do it! First you take off all your clothes! Then you RELAX, and then you twirl and twirl and twirl!"

The journey continues as my native companions and I—now including Dad and thirteen-year-old Will—pitch the large family tent on the back lawn, where we view twinkling stars and tell stories of long, long ago and far, far way until little and medium men are fast asleep, and I, left awake, marvel at the sleeping sweetness of angels and men.

On the final evening of my stay, the family gathers around the table for dinner and Dad asks the familiar question, "Who wants to say the blessing tonight?" As little Charles had already taken a turn the prior evening, a blessing of grand syllabic prose, Joshua loudly claims his turn. "You've got to close your eyes," he insists to us all, and then begins. "Dear God, thank you for this beautiful day, and God, I pray we can stay home forever!"

Donna Runnalls

The Living's Worth…the Being…the Why I…

A quieter world.

Spirit infused lilac purples the mind.
Spirit crystals of light shrouded in morning mist.

Sun rays pitched at an 8 a.m. angle in mid-July
lay a shellac of light on ivy leaves palming the fence line.

His breathing from the other room splintering his dreams.
The breath. The dream.

I think back to the pearlescent breath of my sleeping infant son,
little newt newly arrived from the womb.

Think back to all the sleeping, the breathing,
from other rooms.

Joanna Martin

Under the Big Trees

…there was nothing between me and the white fire of the stars…
–Mary Oliver

It's been forever since I've slept outdoors,
wary now of rattlesnakes, skunks,
mountain lion stories
that roam our neighborhood.

Years ago, when the cabin got claustrophobic,
I'd grab a red-plaid sleeping bag
with no concern or forethought
for any danger that might happen.
I was a middle-aged child
discovering solace under the ancient oak
that leaned over the deck.
Beards of moss draped like black lace
and I couldn't shut my eyes
transfixed by moon and starlight.

My husband, after four years in foxholes,
did not join in my adventures.
We had not yet heard of PTSD.
On a camping trip to Big Sur
he was only too happy
to take our hidden dog home
when the park ranger caught us.
I stayed with the children,
scenting chili with bay leaf.
Serene and content with my own aloneness
and the way my flames burned just fine.

Bernice Rendrick

An Unexpected Transition

At the start of 2020, I had already experienced enough transitions for a couple of lifetimes: from new births to untimely deaths, beautiful vistas to scenes of total destruction, great emotional highs to the depths of despair. I believed that life constantly changed and that, somehow, we had to adapt to each change or drown in the sheer magnitude of them. I felt that I had learned the art of adaptation pretty well. But when challenged with one of the biggest life changes most of us have ever faced, I had no idea that this atypical, unpredictable occurrence would catch me at a loss.

It's one thing to expect to be affected by illness and death in our lives. We can anticipate weddings, funerals, job losses and moves. We can imagine being separated from loved ones temporarily while sick or on vacation. What has caught us so unprepared is that these recent changes have been beyond our scope of experience and our control.

This pandemic-created transition is not in any manual, rulebook or list of guidelines we've learned in school or life. During most of the previous highs and lows of my own life, my family and friends were with me to lend support and comfort.

Now, due to distance and SIP, I have not been able to see much of my family or friends. But what I have learned in the past few months is that having a partner with whom to share the time and isolation is the lifeline that has kept me from going stir-crazy. We can laugh, play, work and even bicker, but it's all good because we have each other.

Laughter, love, and shared concerns are the best antidotes I have found to deal with this very long and unpredictable transition.

Dinah Davis

We Curled Together Nude After Sleep

And found ourselves in the familiar niches.
You were heavy-bodied, dozing,
our breathing settled in rhythm
like atoms entangled
to become one hum.
I felt all the creatures
of the earth curled next to each other,
skin to fur to feather to snout,
bodies warm, groin to backside.
I inhaled you, the faint scent of your sex,
the air was ocean, early morning
midsummer when nothing moves.
Just a quiet lapping of breath —
your life moving up and
down your skin,
your dreams still alive in you.
You turned to your side,
murmuring soft sighs
and I cupped the back of you
like night sky to crescent moon.
Outside the sun was curling
over the redwood tree.
Two mourning doves
rested together at treetop,
before fluttering off —
the music of their wings
fluttering our own eyes awake.
I inhaled your skin,
the rise of your belly
told me life was alive,
it was living, I had it
cupped in my hands.

Carolyn Brigit Flynn

Alive Together

A friend came to dinner last night and lamented not being alive together with her mate of fifty years. She didn't know who she was without him, how could she go on?

That evening, while Dan and I cleaned up the kitchen together, placing the wedding gift wine glasses carefully away, we couldn't conceive of not being alive together. After nearly sixty years, raising children, burying parents, taking vitamins, making music, writing poetry, the years fall away, boulders down the cliff . . .

Falling asleep over books, holding each other, dreams of ancestors come knocking: there's my Bubie Anna throwing feed to the chickens. She died while we were on our honeymoon. Our first daughter was named after her. One by one the beloveds appear, my mother, father, in-laws, aunts, uncles, friends. Gathered into a bouquet, I hold them close.

Journaling in the garden the next morning, red tulips blooming like at our first home in 1969 when second child Caitlin was a baby, I write, "The past bleeds into the present, bringing me to this moment. As long as I'm alive, I will experience whatever they have to offer, with or without my partner."

Over breakfast, I ask Dan if my journals would be a burden to him, should he be the one left behind. "Your journals are you," he says.

Am I really asking what he would be doing with his writing?

We agree we should both be busy finishing our own work and decide what we want to leave behind. We resolved early on to do each other a favor by taking individual responsibility for our personal health. Alive together, we had to learn how to take care and support each other.

Beginning the marriage marathon, odds against us—a shotgun wedding, baby on the way, too young to know better . . . and yet here we are, mostly for the better (we don't remember the worse!). We came together loving life. We learned to love our life together. Alive together or separated, continue we will.

Judy Phillips

Catalogue Ending with a Love

Bend to your given life and it'll rise to meet you.
Yes, that stint in the jail seems unnecessary,
the slick mountain road where you
totaled the Winnebago, scraping the roof
off against the cliff face like those roll top cans
oily with sardines was a bit much. And why
did your second child have to be born
dead inside its mother? Sure, you'd like to
erase your alcoholic Uncle Bob and his
three marriages, undo the petty theft
you were caught for (but keep the others),
but at this distance even they start to shine,
as when you found yourself down on your knees
in the urine-stained bathroom talking to god for the first time
in a long time. The beetle on its back absurdity
of the Winnebago looked like it'd married rock.
The ultrasound showed your baby vogue dancing
with the tube that had once fed it and had now
killed it, wrapped—like a decapitated snake—
around its body. And before Uncle Bob's liver
failed he used to cup his lips around lit matches
to put them out, throw himself into Lake Champlain
from the top of the spindly pine tree that looked
like it'd break under his weight. Take each thing,
polish it with distance, until it too, shines, until
the whole string of disasters and setbacks
are set like pearls on a long chain you lift
from its display case and drape around
the beautiful neck all these rearview mishaps
led you to. Kiss it as the clasp closes, not
from sexual desire, but cockamamie happiness.
She's here because of all you survived, and didn't.

David Sullivan

Soul Mate

"There is something more to come, our hearts a gold mine not yet plumbed,
an uncharted sea." –Dorianne Laux

Who would guess that gawky computer nerd
interviewing me for a tech support job
would shyly seduce, overthrow my resistance,
thoroughly insinuate himself
into every facet of my life,
penetrate emotional armor
like a persistent virus?

There's no one else
with whom I'd rather shelter,
a man who massages an aching shoulder,
empties the dishwasher without being asked,
helps change unwieldy California King sheets.
surprises me with takeout
on nights I don't want to cook,
delivers fragrant bouquets
of my favorite flowers.

Together, we explore territory
my lonesome self would never have tackled:
summer march with striking workers in Paris,
Alicante apartment, bullet train to Madrid,
inner tube ride down Kauai sugar cane plantation ditches,
commutes filled with grief as my mom died of cancer,
chasing iguanas through stone ruins
at Isla de Mujeres and Chichén Itzá.

As a team, we've survived panic attacks,
heart arrhythmias, drug reactions, withdrawals;
discovered online artisan bread or turkey tamale pie recipes,
obscure Netflix movies during pandemic lockdown.
Despite isolation, uncertainty of what's to come,
we still laugh, hold hands, kiss morning and night,
celebrate small triumphs with cheesecake, gelato.

Jennifer Lagier

–photo courtesy of The Homeless Garden Project

Providence

Accretion, accrual—small things becoming
larger, part of, forming their own constructions
or causing current structures to fail or fall.

Small kindnesses add up to a friendship;
discrete, ephemeral days accumulate to a lifetime.
Happenstance engenders relationship.

Dig with a spoon and eventually you have a tunnel.
Those little French fries turn into pounds.
Rubber bands form a ball, bits of scavenged fabric comprise a quilt.

The small thing cannot be overlooked: the termite,
the dripping water, the turn of phrase. Lemons
from a neighbor, books from a friend. A laughing child.

The work of our hearts and lives is made of small things:
one word then another, a warm touch or thought,
small knots in a larger weave of warmth and comfort.

How many seeds make a field, or snips a haircut?
Every effort, repetitive or insignificant in itself,
matters, as all creations matter.

Building our worlds one thought, one stitch,
one cup of coffee, one prayer, one project, a meal at a time,
we abide by the grace of small things.

Melody Culver

Cheetah Love–photo by Deena Metzger

SEEDS
of CHANGE

Naked Athena

le 23 juillet

Mon amour,

There's a video running on tv here in Paris, but in Spanish for some reason. How this woman walked up to federal brownshirts in Portland. Naked. Completely. Stood there open, exposed. They fired tear gas in her direction. She did yoga asanas on the cold hard pavement. Her leg was bleeding.

The press calls her "Naked Athena." Some say she's an exhibitionist. Others, she's taking away from Black Lives Matter, the purpose of the demonstrations. Still others, that maybe she's black, at least in part.

She reminded me of Delacroix's "Liberty Leading the People," here in the Louvre. Or Collier's "Lady Godiva" in that museum in Bristol.

Maybe she's all these. But mostly for me she's also metaphor, perhaps intended, of what it means to be open. To resist and be vulnerable. Stand there totally naked in front of brute force and power. No barriers, bars, protections. Just yourself as you are. Taking it all off and being and doing what you need to do. Completely.

She came. Stood there. She left. No one knows who she is.

I won't forget it — can't think of anyone or anything more honest, completely open.

Here's a picture I took of her on my tv screen. God, I wish I had her courage. And power.

Je t'aime, mon amour. Ecris moi.

Tu me manques,

Toujours

–Mixed Media, Bob Nielsen

Black Lives Matter–drawing, Sarojani Rohan

Sweetgrass thrives at disturbed edges

The indigenous people of America gather it for prayer.

Something sacred thrives in disturbed places, a simple grass. When it is braided and burned, its fragrance of vanilla and warm hay peels back its ordinariness and reveals its sacred quality. The ceremonial burning of sweetgrass is used to purify and clear, filling the space with healing energy. Its fragrance is a trail to heaven, a song for healing. The Native American peoples of this land honor this simple grass. It is with ritual that two people come together to hold and braid it into bundles of sweetness. The burning of the sweetgrass becomes central to transformation, living as it does where disturbance vibrates the soil and air.

We, as a people, have so many disturbed edges. And now it's the disturbed edges that call out, where neglect, repression, and denial live, where balance is off, and sickness and death happen, when disturbance of the status quo is dangerous and inflammatory.

These edges have existed in the US for a very long time, entangled in our foundations and with who we are. Suddenly the fiery ring of disturbed edges flares into the center, erupts, and crashes against the status quo.

Early this morning I drove to the market. The streets were empty and the air was cool and clear. The birds were singing.

As I finished my shopping and stepped out of the store, there, going down 41st Avenue, one after another, the hunkering black-and-white SUVs with red lights flashing. It seemed an endless line of police cars, inside, the closely cropped heads of men dressed in full uniform. It was the funeral line for a murdered young policeman who was ambushed in Ben Lomond. This long line of law enforcement officers from Santa Cruz and all over California were in solemn procession for the life of officer Damon Gutzwiller.

As I watched I imagined another procession. I imagined the long line of heavy police vehicles in procession for George Floyd, for Rayshard Brooks, for Eric Garner, for Michael Brown, for Tamir Rice, Ahmaud Arbery, Philando Castile, Trayvon Martin, for Sandra Bland and Tanisha Anderson.

I imagined the powerful brotherhood of these officers linked in a procession of respect, of grief.

I imagined all the peoples of USA traveling in the procession, walking, heads bent or lifted high, in grief, burdened by our history and our lineage of slavery and genocide, calling out the names, and calling out the nameless who died as slaves, the calling a trail to heaven, the burning sweetgrass of respect and healing.

Those who have been pushed to the edge become the ground for healing, names spoken into braided song.

The black and-white-vehicles, our blackness and our whiteness, now lit up with flashing red, the smoke of sweetgrass replacing tear gas.

Here in this moment, in this eruption of grief, of anger, now central, we find something sacred to make prayer, to drop to one knee with head bowed in acknowledgement, in our seeing.

Colin Kaepernick took a knee during the national anthem in 2016 and became a disturbed edge, disturbing the NFL, disturbing the white males, disturbing his employment, ostracized to the edges. He said, "I'm not going to stand . . . for the flag of a country that oppresses black people and people of color."

Derek Chauvin took a knee. He held his knee to the throat of a black man, until he cried out for breath and his mother, until George Floyd died. Chauvin is chauvinism on the throat of black Americans. And suddenly thousands take a knee with bent heads all over the world, in the streets, in Congress, for eight minutes and forty-six seconds. Kaepernick's gesture of resistance becomes central, redeemed, the world turns inside out, the wounds erupt. They burn and smoke, splitting the air with calls for justice.

It took four years for the NFL to transform and acknowledge Kaepernick, as thousands dropped to knee after George Floyd's death. Kaepernick, like a shaman, traveled into the disturbed edges to activate the healing.

There's something that thrives on disturbed edges. It's used for healing. Its ordinariness veils its extraordinariness. The extraordinariness of this moment, African Americans taking to the streets with courage and determination, the killing fields fueling their resistance during a deadly pandemic, joined by people of all colors. I imagine them gathering the sweetgrass at the disturbed edges of the fields, singing names, singing the spirituals and songs of freedom from long ago, trails to heaven cutting open denial to the soul of the matter. Gathering the sweetgrass, shaking it and turning it into braids of black and white and red, the red of spilled blood and rage, the red of genocide, the red of all repressed peoples, the red of awakening, braiding it for the remembering of who we are, braiding it into our bones for courage, asking us to take that which has grown at the edges into our hands, into our hearts and let the burning of it open our eyes.

Susan Heinz
June 2020

Sweetgrass grows in places that are along disturbed edges, so writes Robin Wall Kimmerer in her memoir, Braiding Sweetgrass.

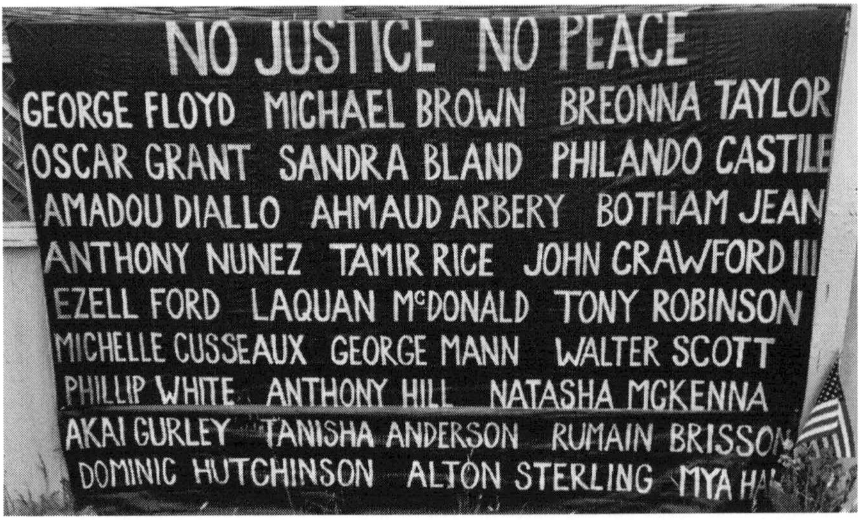

–photo, Kate Aver Avraham, street sign, Aptos CA

Remembering George Floyd

Today I went to the Abandoned Car Lot to find myself a new car.

The man there offered me an old rusty red convertible. He told me it had a low-riding undercarriage because it had carried so much weight in its day. I told him that worked well for me as I would also be carrying a heavy load and I needed a car that could handle it.

"It no longer has a moveable roof," the man explained, "and the windows are permanently down and open to the elements."

"No problem," I said. "Where I'm coming from, the winds that blow show no mercy and the rain seems to pour unendingly.
No problem."

"This is a car nobody's ever seemed to want," he said. "No charge if you'll take it."

"No problem," I said. We slowly pulled out of the lot together, that old red car and I.

I am driving the Car of Compassion. The Driver is Willingness... The Navigator is Courage and the Passengers, Hatred and Violence. They have permanent backseats.

We were there, too, when you took your last breath. There was no sigh of relief, none for you and none for us. You did not die in vain.

Donna Runnalls

Tree of Life
Kaddish for Dr. Jerry Rabinowitz

It's a form of praying,
to hold the darkness inside yourself
and embrace it
the way you would hold water
in a flowing river.

To wake up
with tears flowing from a dream y
our face a field
of milkweed
as the pods scatter
in a wind of prayer
embracing the growing cold.

I remember where he sat
by the window
at the bottom of the flood plain
where the rivers emptied
into the streets that afternoon.
Fire trucks creating a wake
as they moved through the water.

And when the bullets came
he ran toward the shattering souls,
following his instincts
always to help,
to heal the wounded
and the dying.

His friends hold each other
reaching out through time
and a dark river —
holding seeds planted long ago
by the Tree of Life,
say Kaddish in front of an open
Ark of the Covenant.

He would want you to find your light
and embrace it again,
to walk back into the forest
we call the world.

Hold his memory
the way you would hold his face.
Let his voice ripple
through time.
Where the trunk of a redwood tree
thick with the rings of centuries
was burned by lightning,
shine your light
into the dark world.

Diane Frank

I wrote "Tree of Life" four days after the synagogue shooting in Pittsburgh. My dear friend, Dr. Jerry Rabinowitz, was one of the people who lost their lives that day. My poem was the basis of an orchestral piece composed by Matthew Arnerich and performed by the Golden Gate Symphony. Writing this poem and performing the music was a major part of my healing. -DF

these days

give me the bare bones raw and bleeding
the hungry and the grieving
as i want to know it all
i'll even listen to the liars and haters
ya know their plans are only theirs
if i turn away it is only for the moment
as hope is embedded in truth.

barbara weigel

–photo, Nina Koocher, Santa Cruz CA

The Crowd

Pope Francis looks frail,
enters the cathedral
up marble steps.
Prepares to serve mass.
At 78, under his robes and hats he
could just collapse...for days
he stoically keeps going
to parades, blesses children, prays,
gives speeches to the masses.
Waves right, then left.

Meanwhile Bumgarner
fills another stadium,
sails the baseball
through his usual 7 innings.

CEO Mark Zuckerberg
and his wife are expecting, quietly
donate millions to Planned Parenthood.

Everyone believes in something:
Buddha, Jesus Christ, baseball,
Facebook, Obama...

Light is strong this morning,
prints patterns on walls
in mysterious ways.
Leaves, trees, a passing bird.
Art we try to replicate.

In my community Pedro Garcia
notices in the 5 a.m. dark—
cars dodge something on the road.
Stops his bus, blocks traffic,
races to grab the lost toddler.

I believe in all of this—
our human ways that bind us
as we strive for a goodness
where we can all fit in, perhaps
be rescued when we need it.

Bernice Rendrick
2015

A Time for Listening–painting, Susan Heinz, *March 2020*

Not Hope but Possibility

I am thinking of the possibilities for a future for this poor beleaguered planet Earth. I am heartbroken. I do not have hope. Sometimes hope is an obstacle to the offering that is necessary. I don't hope, but I recognize and respond to possibility. What are the possibilities that we might change the dire situation we are in?

What are the possibilities? Which ones call to us? How will we meet them?

Holding these questions is how I live. I go on because I am living the possibilities every day and such a life is focused, full of energy and determination. When I see that you are living the possibilities too then I am enthusiastic. It may not matter, ultimately, if we will succeed, for who can define success? It matters, inordinately, that we are each, in all the ways open to, determined to meet the times.

For too many years, I have been writing about meeting Extinction, Climate Dissolution and Social and Political Chaos. I capitalize these words because they are so large and this is what we are up against. The lights are going out. I don't want to diminish in any way the dire circumstances that confront us and all life.

And to be truthful, I have no patience for those who say, they can't face it all because they get too depressed and then they can't function. To them I say, tell that to Polar Bear mother whose ice, the land she needs to survive, is melting because of how we live and she and her cubs are starving. Tell that to Elephant mother, to the Matriarch who is responsible for the entire herd but can't find water or food and if/when she does, finally, the poachers descend and cut off her tusks while she is still alive and her calves are watching. Tell that to the Wolf pack which is running from the helicopters with marksmen shooting AK47s at them. This hunt is to protect the cows from the wolves so humans can eat cow while the wolf pups will die of hunger without a pack to sustain them. Their situation is grim and they are helpless before us. We are not helpless and so we cannot look away.

There is an enormous energy—infinite possibilities—that come from bearing witness and living accordingly. These are two actions that must be one—bear witness and live accordingly. Change your life. Let your heart guide you. Become an ethical being. It is so very difficult and so very simple. Bear witness and change your lives accordingly.

There are so many possibilities I consider each day, week, month, year; there are no end to them. So today, I would like to offer one that has been preoccupying me for some years and one that is particularly apt for us here: Seeds of change lie in literature. A new literature can help create a viable world. Let's imagine being participants in a Literature of Restoration.

I was planning to write a formal essay on the subject in preparation for focusing all my writing circles on the Literature of Restoration. But I don't want to offer a formal essay here. —Actually, that would not accord with a Literature of Restorations, as form determines content. Instead, I would like to muse with you about this possibility, hopefully engaging your curiosity and willingness to explore this with me. Frankly, I would like to seduce you into taking on the challenge: Let's save Planet Earth.

Planet Earth. Let's give Her her due first. Earth Mother. Let's not battle to save Her. Rather let's see what we can gather from all dimensions so that we feel deep alliance with Her and so protective of her, so thoughtful about how we act in relationship to her, that we are taken, by the power of language, our own words, into that relationship which is profoundly sustaining and revives the connections which all lives depend upon. Magic? Of course. Just saying these words immediately creates a different environment that supports change. Going to the trenches, entering a battle on behalf of her, warring for her, no matter the outcome, changes nothing. The one who wars, whose mind is at war when provoked is the one who, ultimately, does harm. But the lover seeds life. But make no mistake, deep loving can be gritty, fierce and very challenging.

Rather than a Literature based on conflict, I am suggesting that we find the magnetic center of what we are writing and let it attract the necessary stories, events, experiences to it. That we give up all imposed formulae and arbitrary categories and limiting definitions and let the writing itself, the muse, the stories, the characters enact the context in which they want to live and flourish. Let's give up thinking we're in charge or ought to be. Let's yield to the spirits, and see what they want to say and how. Let's see if we can create interdependent, complex, diverse, cooperating and nourishing forms that mirror the Earth's ecological, interlacing, interdependent ways.

I am thinking of the eros of resonance rather than contemporary literature's obsession with violence. A Literature which is a peacemaker rather than a warmonger. Let's see what brings us together rather than what pulls us apart. If English offers us anything in this area, it offers us metaphor. Let's see where metaphor can take us. Metaphor—the lightning of understanding that strikes when two unlikely, or very distinct elements, align and create something new— sperm and egg, pollen and nuclei leading to life and beauty. Let's reverse extinction and climate collapse through literature emerging from our own hands.

A Literature of Restoration because it leads to restoration. Because it honors the old, old ways, the Indigenous Earth-based, Spirit-based values, by including them in the text. Because such a literature references the ancestors instead of commercial brands, because it identifies the Earth, location, the ground from which it springs, rather than what is manufactured, because it honors soul instead of economics, such literature by its nature restores us to a sane world.

This Literature can be a Council, honoring the myriad voices, seeking diversity, multiplicity, differences. Because the other in such texts can be seen as kin instead of enemy, the possibilities of revelation and deep understanding increases. A Literature that is a circle, not a straight line, that honors the curve of poetry and not only the straight line of reasoning, that drops the false barriers that imprison writing in a box, that does not ask us for word count or pretend to know what a story is or isn't, what a novel is and why it isn't memoir, how many pages a screenplay needs to be (120 preferred) and on which page the climax occurs, but gives us permission to become everything we might be, a fertile field, a fecund jungle, a babbling brook rather than a tower of Babel, a night sky full of points of light. Song. Which light do we prefer—the fluorescent display of urban commerce or the darkness which lets you see light years away to the faintest beginnings?

Let all the barriers come down, dissolve the categories, let history, dream and fiction coexist, the past and present intermingle, the known and unknowable interpenetrating. Write the complex and fluid continuous present, allow the animals to enter and leave a text as they might traverse the field where we are standing unafraid of the life that abounds there. Allow even the assumption of human hegemony, human superiority to crumble. Imagine a literature that is truly homo-centric without being human-centric. Let's hear it all.

Not an easy Literature. But proposing radically truthful telling. And ethics. Rigorous ethics that we live first and foremost before they reach the page. Refusing to diminish or belittle what must be seen and reckoned with. A Literature with an adamant gaze. Bearing witness, unflinchingly but with anguish, pain, grief and heartbreak. Imagination without pretense. Wild visions without consoling fantasies.

Imagine such a Literature which by its morphing and fractal shapes, by its refusal to be cut off from the past or the future, by its insistence on including the vastness and particularity of the imagination, by saying yes and yes and yes, allows all the life-forms to coexist in dynamic relationship. Imagine such a possibility, such possibilities from our pens.

And finally, prayer. A literature that allows prayer.

Great Spirit, Great Heart, Great Mystery, Awesome Presence, Ancestors and Future Beings. Thank you for Your Presence in our lives. Thank you for our lives. May we find the words that are needed in these times. May we have the language to speak what must be spoken. May all the stories that need to be told, be told. May we not hold back what needs to be made visible. May we have the courage to look at everything without denying the terrible truths of our lives. May we have insight and vision. May we discover the language of the heart. May our words be true and may they be courageous. May the Earth be restored. May there be viable futures for all beings and may our words help bring such possibilities to life.

Aho.

Deena Metzger

One Potato

So I say to you, walk with the wind, brothers and sisters, and let the spirit of peace and the power of everlasting love be your guide. –John Lewis

Yesterday morning, I listened to the celebration of John Lewis's life and wept; not only because he's gone, but because of who our current leaders are not. His many sacrifices moved the needle but not as far as we had hoped. We still have a steep climb ahead.

In the afternoon, my listening day was bookended by a riff from Noam Chomsky on *Democracy Now!* I cried again: *maybe* fifteen years until the Amazon rainforest becomes a carbon-emitter rather than a carbon sink; nuclear treaties scrapped and a renewed arms race under reckless despots here in the U.S., Russia, China, and likely Saudi Arabia, Israel and India; tens of millions of people starving now or soon; the pandemic and the plastics and the dithering. Our pockets are full of problems. Our basket of options is nearly empty.

We seem to have forgotten how spellbound we were back in March, as we watched the resurgence of the natural world during the pandemic lockdown. Climate restoration is hardly on the radar anymore as we rush to find a panacea in the form of a vaccine without addressing the root causes of our ills—the poisoning of the natural world, the decimation of the systems that sustain life; the torment of the vulnerable. We continue to chase quick fixes as if we didn't know better.

As the world spirals, the questions have not changed, though they grow more urgent: In the face of all that is happening, how to respond? What to do and say? How to sing our great yearning? My Liberian brother, Bill Saa, says, *If I am healed, I can heal twenty people just by interacting with them; each of them can heal twenty; each of them can heal twenty more. That's the way it works.* If this is true, or, perhaps, since this is true, then we must take our task to heart—to heal ourselves as best we can by learning to love so well that we, and the world, are transformed.

On election night, 2016, I was at the Intertribal Conversations in New Mexico, a biannual gathering of Native American changemakers from across the U.S. and beyond. It was perplexing: no one mentioned the election. Not one word, before or after. My curiosity got the better of me, and I finally asked why. The young man in charge looked at me with great, pitying kindness, and said, *Well, put it this way: we've been screwed for the last five hundred years, and we're still screwed now. For us, it makes no difference who's in the White House. Our work doesn't change.* I heard the same thing from Palestinian peacebuilders in the West Bank: *If we allowed one toxic individual to take us down, we would have given up long ago.* During the Troubles, Joe Campbell, a peacebuilder from Northern Ireland, once told me, *I'm here to make a difference in my time.*

And so I've been wondering about this business of *walking with the wind;* of *the work doesn't change;* of how we can each *make a difference in our time.* And I think of my friend, Susan Cerulean, a splendid writer who is devoted to birds, particularly the shorebirds of northern Florida along the Gulf of Mexico, near Tallahassee, where she lives. She bears witness to human encroachment and its toll on the tiny, essential, feathered wizards who struggle to survive. Her book has just been published: *I Have Been Assigned the Single Bird: A Daughter's Memoir.* It's the parallel story of caring for her dying father as he struggled with dementia while trying to protect the endangered plover, the bird she adores above all. She says,

> *The Earth is the brain and the body into which we were born...*
> *I offer you the story of my own explorations in service to this*
> *question: How can we care for this world? I have tried to*

reconcile my roles as one daughter caring for one father, as one woman
attuned at times to only a single wild bird while the planet is burning. How I long to change the world for the better. Offering care to those we love is closely similar to standing up for our Earth. In all cases, we are required to be fierce and full-bodied advocates in an endless series of small actions, each as important as the next. This story braids the human and the animal, as it must, for we can never be separate.

Last night, unsettled by sadness, I puttered aimlessly in the kitchen. I looked closely at some potatoes harvested from my garden—one potato, in particular. By the time it was pulled from the soil, it was no longer edible. Its skin is leathery. Shriveled. Its wrinkles look like an elephant hide. But here's the thing: it's sprouting! Its last dying act is to give itself completely to feeding new life. Last night, there were six sprouts. Today, there are seven. Tomorrow, who knows? A nursery rhyme comes to mind: *One potato, two potato, three potato, four. Five potato, six potato, seven potato more.* As the dying potato shrinks until it disappears, it empties itself into new life, as we must empty ourselves into a livable future. What do we feed with our lives? My task is to put those sprouting potatoes in good soil, to water and tend them with care. The same with the ways I tend my words, and all that I love. My prayer is that I learn to feed them well, knowing that we and the future will be fed in return.

Cynthia Travis

I Leave You Love–Nancy Jones, Mixed Media Series 2020,
For the 100th Anniversary of Women's Right to Vote
Photo credit: Florida Memory, Daytona Beach

I leave you love. I leave you hope. I leave you the challenge of developing confidence in one another. I leave you a thirst for education. I leave you a respect for power. I leave you faith. I leave you racial dignity. I leave you a desire to live harmoniously with your fellow man. I leave you finally a responsibility to our young people.

—Mary McLeod Bethune, Educator, 1875-1955

Changing Our Minds
The call of initiation in a collapsing world

How do we change our minds? I don't mean making a decision and then choosing to decide something else, though that may be a part of things. I mean how do we allow the matrix of understanding that has ordered and explained our world to become something else? When I say mind, I don't just mean our thoughts, I mean the entire constellation of assumptions, thoughts, habits, external and internal structures that hold in place how we inhabit our world; what water is to a fish or air to a bird, for example. This web that holds our living is often so internalized, so much a part of the autonomic nervous system of how we go about our days that most of the time we don't recognize or even know it's there. And because we are mostly unaware of it, we rarely, if ever, question it. It just is.

Until it doesn't work anymore. We wake up feeling empty morning after morning, or we get ill, or we lose our job, or someone we cherish dies, or we have a vague, persistent recognition that our life isn't working even if we can't articulate what that means. The catalysts for change are legion. Sometimes the impetus is internal; we've just had enough of whatever it is and we know that a new way is calling even if we have no idea what that is. Many times the source of change comes from a force outside ourselves, something often frightening or unwelcome, that comes crashing or seeping into our life. We are left bereft, undone and no longer know how to live.

Such change comes not only to individuals, it comes also to families, communities, organizations, institutions, countries and cultures. I have come to call such radical disruption of our world initiation. It means that the scaffolding that has held us together is crumbling so that a new way of being can be born. It is the process of moving from one way of being and thinking to another. It means letting go of what isn't working, even as much as we may have a certain affection for it because it is familiar, helps order our days or perhaps invites fond memories of how life used to be. It means letting go of what we know, even when we have no earthly idea of what will come next. It means living in a shaky, unmoored reality for however long it takes for a life o dissolve with no idea if a new one will take its place. Most of us do not choose this willingly.

It is also why such a process often becomes a central story in religious and spiritual tradition. It is the Israelites leaving Egypt and wandering in the desert for forty years in hopes of finding the promised land. It is Jesus in the wilderness for forty days, or in the tomb for three. It is Inanna in the underworld. It is the Tower card of the Tarot eventually giving way to the Star of destiny. It is Persephone gone below, the seemingly interminable barren landscape, going through the motions of existing before new life emerges. It is the stuff of poetry and song, epic tales and the bard's lament. And that all means that we have lots of help. Lots of people have traveled this road before us and they know something about pointing the way.

Here we are. For roughly six months, the globe has been upended by the coronavirus. The entire human rhythm of the world has been suspended as we create and follow measures to stay safe and healthy if we are privileged to do so; as we grieve the loss of those dear to us who are dying without us by their side; as we see our businesses go under before our eyes and wonder how our towns will survive the crush of unemployment.

All this, of course, is taking place when the planet is heating up at an unprecedented rate, accelerating species loss and threatening the very existence of our future on earth. Climate scientists reported earlier this year that up to one-third of animal and plant species could become extinct in fifty years. Meanwhile, the West Coast wildfires this season have burned more acreage than any other time in recorded history, while drought and floods continue to devastate other regions around the globe.

The time has come: We who are human are in initiation.

Then on May 25th George Floyd was murdered by a cop with his knee on his neck choking the breath out of him while he begged for his life; one life in a long, long line of black and brown lives choked or beaten or shot or knifed or lynched because of the color of their skin. And then it all boiled over—not one life, or one year, but centuries of the white knee on the black neck, ever since 1619 when the first slave ship landed on these now American shores—no air, no life, no rest for 401 years on this soil.

The first settlers in this country arrived in 1607 and 1620, in Jamestown, VA and Plymouth, MA, respectively. The wash of colonialism that followed forced the original people of this land off the earth of their ancestors, while their languages, customs and people were systematically met with attempted eradication.

These are the legacies our country stands on. The time has come: We who are white are in initiation, and we are in it whether we welcome it or not.

In the dream I am standing on a headland looking out over the vast sea. Behind me is my house, a rambling white stucco structure with vines of roses growing wildly. On the horizon to my right I see the deep dark clouds of a storm brewing. It is coming my way. I start to run away from the headland towards the woods when the architect of my house calls out. "Don't flee. Stay." I return to the house where the architect points to a large box in the center. "You must ride out the storm inside here," the voice says. I climb in.

When the scene shifts, the storm has passed over. Most of my house has been destroyed – only a few upright studs remain, but the box I have now stepped out of is gleaming gold.

When this dream arrived in my twenties, I was in my own initiation. My life, or my house, was crumbling around me as the storm of physical pain began to make it impossible for me to pursue my dream of becoming a professional musician. It took many years to recognize that a bright life, or in the language of the dream, the gold box, could still rise from the devastation.

This is the language of initiation: the winds of change come upon us, our familiar dwellings of thought, habit and assumptions are often ravaged, yet even in the midst of the raging chaos, we are asked by the architect of life not to flee. We are invited instead into staying power, into the arduous, often long, long work of regarding what needs to crumble and then letting it go, all the while living without a vision of the new life that wants to be given a chance. When the storm swirls around us, we have no idea if the inner sanctum we are laboring in will shine brightly or not. If that sounds hard, it is. It is why, so often, the change comes upon us seemingly uninvited. I say "seemingly" because, somewhere deep in the force called life is the willing spark of revolutionary desire, the often-hidden place where the possibility of a life more just, more beautiful, more sustaining of all creation "lives and moves and has its being."

Initiation begins when the life we are living is too small for the life that wants to be lived through us. But how do we live when much of what we know and the rhythms that have ordered our days are crumbling? Initiation is a time of slowing down, a time given to the moment by moment listening and then responding to the deeper voices of direction within and beyond us. Sometimes guidance is given in our dreams. We wake and then enter into meditation or dialogue with a being or situation that has come in our sleep, attending to how the night time story is instructing us. We take a slow walk in the woods, allowing ourselves to be drawn to the rocks, the trees, the animals that beckon us to quiet our minds so that they may speak wisdom without words. We meditate, understanding that practicing staying power is needed medicine for these times. We gather in community to bear witness, seek courage and listen together. Beauty and wildness, stillness and quiet, solitude and community are the landscapes that call us to become nimble, to let go, to pay attention and stay curious even as our familiar ways dissolve around us.

Initiation is soul time with surprising gifts, not the least of which is the unshakable knowing that we are not the only intelligence guiding a life. We are profoundly and generously taught and accompanied by a multidimensional world where animals, elements, the ancestors and sometimes the seemingly unbelievable synchronicities of life offer themselves to a life of shared creation, direction and wonder.

Before a caterpillar becomes a butterfly, it enters the "goo," the stage where its body goes fully into solution before the butterfly emerges. We as a country and a world have been taken into the goo. We are long overdue for a new mind. The old ways of human hegemony and white supremacy have got to go. But as Audre Lorde cautioned us years ago, "The master's tools will never dismantle the master's house." We cannot do that work from the old mind.

Thus, we are taken into initiation. The scaffolding will buckle around us. We won't know where to turn. Institutions will crumble. We will grieve the comforts of old habits of life, as diminishing as they have become or as death-dealing as they always were. We won't know what tomorrow will look like. We won't be able to make plans. And all of that is absolutely essential.

But we are not without guidance. An intelligence awaits. An intimacy awaits. We can allow ourselves to be instructed by a wisdom that has come before us and lives ahead of us. Life is waiting. She's here in the thick of it, unformed, unrelenting and often invisible, but calling to us nonetheless. The ancestors and the future beings of our world are waiting.

Lawrie Hartt

The Force

Outside, eerie orange sky,
clogged with smoke and ash,
sun snuffed out, air frigid and
as dark as when locusts swarmed
over Pharaoh's realm.

One could believe
the end of the world is near.
Or that evil beings in the east
who speak with forked tongues,
have cursed us the way Darth Vader
challenged Skywalker's fight for good.

Maybe this is how Mars became
the dead red planet. Martians forgot
to protect their environment.
Deception, greed for material things
mushroomed into a great gray
cloud of toxic depravity.

Earthlings, it's still not too late.
Keep your light sabers on hand,
glowing and humming...

May the force be with you.

Kate Aver Avraham

INTO the GREAT MYSTERY

Flight–Mixed Media, Sara Friedlander
From the series Offerings: Human/Nature #1

Waking Up

I wake inside a dream so real—the convoluted house with secret rooms,
The people I know but don't belong there,
The task that never gets done . . .
Sometimes the dream is filled with lavender and hyacinth,
And I can float above it all,
And all day I remember the feeling of flying,
But when I finally wake from those nighttime dreams,
I find myself in another dream, the one inside my head.
It is all there, the people, the names of things, the convoluted plans
    and schedules,
The tasks that will never get done.
Then I stop, there at my kitchen table,
And I wake up again and know I have been dreaming again.
Outside there is a red-tailed hawk, seated high on his throne of a branch,
        royal in his dominion over the earth,
        his russet shoulders, epaulettes,
        his keen eye and keen hunger single-minded and alert.
Hawk, tree, my categories, my brain's neat pockets.
There is only hawking and treeing going on
And now the transmogrified mouse—soaring.
Wake up I say.
Stay awake for this, today's show.
Let the plans happen and the tasks be done,
But don't miss your life. Don't let your miracle of a being, you, nature
    awakening
To itself, sleep through the days you have remaining.
This is how it begins, this waking up.
It begins with noticing.
That's all there is to it.
Paying attention.
And abandoning all the lies we have believed.
So let us begin.

Dennis Hamilton

Break the Mirror

Forget what you look like
and lean into the unrelenting curve
that pulls the earth around the sun.
Surrender to the wildness
of your own aging
as ancient curves pull day into night
and coax the land from summer into autumn.

You were only lent to this world,
and your home will want you back one day.
Put away your brush and comb now,
let the rings drop off your fingers.
Practice your return
if you truly desire the perfect end
you pray for.

Don't look into the river for your rippling reflection.
Step from the shore and dive into its current.
As this water knows its path
to the depths of the sea,
so your wild aging heart
knows your way
into the great mystery.

Mary Camille Thomas

Any Common Desolation

can be enough to make you look up
at the yellowed leaves of the apple tree, the few
that survived the rains and frost, shot
with late afternoon sun. They glow a deep
orange-gold against a blue so sheer,
a single bird would rip it like silk. You may have to break
your heart, but it isn't nothing
to know even one moment alive. The sound
of an oar in an oarlock or a ruminant
animal tearing grass. The smell of grated ginger.
The ruby neon of the liquor store sign.
Warm socks. You remember your mother,
her precision a ceremony, as she gathered
the white cotton, slipped it over your toes,
drew up the heel, turned the cuff. A breath
can uncoil as you walk across your own muddy yard,
the big dipper pouring night down over you, and everything
you dread, all you can't bear, dissolves
and, like a needle slipped into your vein—
that sudden rush of the world.

Ellen Bass
from Indigo
Copper Canyon Press, 2020

Strike Up the Band

Attend to each thing that this world offers,
balm for sorrows. Always, in front of you,
stacked crates of fruit just starting to lean to
as their pyramids rise behind the market.
A man with no hair is graced with a length
of beard that spirals down to his sunk chest
as if kissing both nipples. The toddler
wing-flaps his arms to chase down a blackbird.
The woman holds one arm in the other,
as if she were injured—perhaps she is—
but the arm is like an infant she can't
release. Each waits for you to notice them,
so they can come alive, do their given dance.
Your job is to open up. Give them a chance.

David Sullivan

Paying Attention

It means to peel a grape and press the texture of its flesh against your tongue, feel the juice trickle down your throat as you squish it between your teeth, remember its sweetness before you drift to sleep.

It means to draw a schematic in your mind of the maze created by rats above your bedroom ceiling by listening to how they scurry, tear through insulation, bite through wiring, make their home in the world, not unlike what you have done.

It means to be able to predict temperature by how early in the morning central heating begins to whir, blows warming air and dust around the room, invokes a sneeze.

It means to watch how the black squirrel at the bird feeder dominates the brown squirrel, flicks a claw at its nose to secure a prime position in the tray, see how it stuffs its cheeks with seed and suet, wraps its tail around its back and points toward the sky.

It means recognizing every ingredient in Bittersweet Bistro's paella, letting the rice drenched in saffron seep in, the simmered prawns curl into themselves in pink splendor, the zing of spicy chorizo erupt, tomatoes and bell peppers and onion showcasing the garden, the paprika and garlic and parsley infusing everything.

It means knowing that to attend, you are required to pay, whether in bills and coins, minutes and days, prioritizing the available storage space in your brain, choosing carefully how to spend your time, your life, as if it's the only one you'll ever get.

Jory Post

33

A month ago there was a distressed hawk flying low, shrieking all day and into the evening. A neighbor told us not to worry, that it was only a juvenile hawk "sorting himself out." He must be sorted now as there is quiet in the skies with only the occasional familiar call of the adult red-tails circling slowly over.

When I find myself caught in a living-death-by-a-thousand-administered distractions, I wonder if it might help if I also started circling around; "Not to worry, she's just sorting herself out."

Now that I am at a point in my life where both the beginning and the end horizons are visible, I do have many things sorted: I do not want to die by distraction or to-do lists; I cherish silence; I don't like it when I am mean. I get it about kindness: "It is a bit embarrassing to have been concerned with the human problem all one's life and find at the end that one has no more to offer by way of advice than, 'Try to be a little kinder.'" I know that kindness is a worthy practice for an individual as well as a nation. I also know that true kindness has teeth.

Lauren Crux
Excerpt from "Little Rambles"

Pogonip Path–photo, Sara Friedlander

In the beginning I went for a walk each day, needing to be outdoors and in nature, with the ever-present thought that others were confined indoors and I might record the coming of spring for them to experience. At the same time I was pulled back into making ceramics after working on a photo project over the last year. I've probably hand-built thirty tea bowls since the pandemic forced us to retreat inside. And that, too, has helped me stay centered and grounded so that I can do the political activism that seems urgent, if we are to continue in our struggle for justice on every front. -SF

What Do We Know?

The poetry ancestors scattered to all parts of the world. Each family of trees, animals, winds, stones needed a poet.

—Joy Harjo, *Conflict Resolution for Holy Beings*

On the beach in Santa Barbara years ago, walking with a friend from Liberia, a ripple of ocean washed over our feet and tumbled some small stones at the water's edge. One of the stones tipped onto its rim. As it did so, it became briefly translucent: the late afternoon sun shone through it and transformed it into a shimmering green window, an oval of stained glass. We turned to each other, excited and grinning.

"It's alive!" my friend exclaimed.

A moment later, it lay flat, "merely" a stone again. We wondered, could this have occurred with any stone or was this one special? At the time, I thought that particular stone was different. I brought it home, wanting to keep its miracle close. (I later returned it.) Now, I would say all stones are alive. What does this understanding require of me in the ways I behave and speak?

Yesterday, a friend shared a dream of seeing a bear just on the other side of a low patio fence of a home in a rural area where bears were once ubiquitous and now are rare. The bear in the dream was calm, peering with gentle curiosity into the garden. If one loves bears, and the wild, as many of us do, this dream merits a thoughtful response. What might such a response be? How would it shape us?

Last week, a friend told me of his brother's recent suicide, which led to involvement with a suicide prevention organization. The head of that initiative is a suicide survivor. A couple of years ago, he jumped off the Golden Gate bridge. A bystander called 911. As the man hit the water, he did not die, though he was seriously injured, with several broken bones. But he thought, "I will *not* die now!" Then he saw a dark shape circling him, and he thought, "I will *not* be killed by a shark!" But it wasn't a shark, it was a sea lion. The sea lion swam under him and lifted him to the surface and kept him afloat until the Coast Guard arrived. That story went deep; for days, I couldn't shake it. I didn't want to. I was so grateful for its company. When I shared it in a recent circle, one friend said, "How can a story like that not change everything?"

Here's what I know: Dreams are more reliable than minds. Synchronicities are more reliable than facts. Experience is more reliable than data. Here in the U.S., the dreams that are coming now contain great teachings about right relationship. What are dreamers dreaming in India? In Yemen? In the slums of Nairobi?

It is time to be guided by something deeper than data or theory or expertise.

Inexplicable synchronous events reveal patterns, directives, and mysteries worth exploring. Unexpected connection engenders delight and a kind of reverence that insists that we find deeper ways to tend to the unseen world from which the most reliable guidance consistently comes. I didn't grow up reverent. The inexplicable has taught me and I am still learning.

~

The I Ching speaks of the "smallest possible gesture" required to solve a problem. If such a gesture is aligned with the Way—with the larger rhythms we can only glimpse—it changes fate. Tempting as it is to focus on the big stuff, and seek the sweeping changes required to birth a new time, perhaps this is a medicinal moment to start with the small.

I think about the "butterfly effect"—the flap of a butterfly's wings in a cloud forest that sets something in motion, a subtle movement of air that brings a downpour. Of course, the butterfly is just being itself, with no thought for whether or when to flap its wings and seemingly little notion of the consequences. That, too, is a gift: a knowing-how-to-be that contributes to unified balance. Then again, perhaps it would be better to assume that it's all intentional, that every living being has agency that deserves our meticulous respect.

Each of us has experienced the divine in our own way. It is time to live what our bodies know to be true, and to consider how to deliver the gifts we were given in the time we are allotted. In the midst of the pandemic and its implications, the question of how to live has taken on a new and multifaceted urgency: how to stay alive, and protect those that we love, human and other-than-human; and how, in Joy Harjo's words, to live the stories "trembling with fresh life."

How has it happened that under our watch the world became so ill? The great and perilous gift of this moment is that the entire human race has been forced to stop and consider how to protect Life. Recently a friend spoke of his anguish at feeling that, despite the carefully curated intentions and actions that have shaped his work, he feels he has failed to deliver, to be effective in what he came here to do. Sometimes, it helps to think less about solutions and more about the conditions needed for thriving. I think of the expression, to *amend* the soil before planting. What amends must be made, what new bonds forged? What is the deep knowing that has burnished each of us, but that we may have hesitated—until now—to act from? There is a pollinator-friendly garden to seed at this time: how do we prepare the soil of ourselves?

Cynthia Travis

A Map to the Kingdom

Let me draw myself a map
out of the world of scarcity
into the kingdom
where everyone has enough.

The map I'm talking about
requires a subtle yet revolutionary algorithm
to rewrite the neuronal pathways of my brain.
Let my ears hear the soft call to prayer
from the cave of my heart
instead of the 21st-century symphonic blast
begging me to worship at the altar of the mall
and buy more apps for my iPhone.
The promise of productivity
and the buzz of news and games
want to trick me into believing
they can fill me up and give me purpose.

But no.
Rewire the neurons.
Let me rejoice in the gift of each moment
instead of fretting about what I don't have time for.
Then I can find the cartographers
who will collaborate with me
in mapping our way to the kingdom of enough.
In that place time is the currency,
and communion is all we want to buy.

Mary Camille Thomas

The Lion and the Light

Cast all your anxiety on God, because God cares for you. Like a roaring lion your evil adversary prowls around, looking for someone to devour. Resist him, for you know that your brothers and sisters throughout the world are undergoing the same kinds of suffering. —I Peter 5:7-9

A few years ago, a friend and I traveled to Tanzania and, partnering with the Mother's Union, delivered solar ovens to women in rural villages. Mission complete, we hired a driver and instead of heading to the north to the Serengeti, we opted to go south, where tourists rarely ventured. On our first night in Ruaha State Park, we ate dinner outside on the lower viewing deck closest to a watering hole, where a family of elephants were drinking and bathing. As darkness settled, we heard lions, their roars getting closer. A staff member appeared at the edge of the deck frantically waving a flashlight. He explained that the perimeter flood lights, that keep the lions at bay, failed, but a flashlight worked in a pinch! Now, whenever I'm facing my personal "roaring lions," I remember how a small flashlight in the African night kept me safe.

These quarantine months sometimes feel like a lion is prowling in the darkness of the unknown, of fear, isolation, depression and anxiety. It's a deadly, invisible enemy but is powerful enough to shut down the entire globe, to kill over 550,000 people and plunder every economy on earth. Still, this little light of mine...and yours...can illuminate the darkness with enough love and laughter, kindness and generosity to wreak havoc on the coronavirus. Our light can lift spirits, give hope, restore, support, and strengthen.

In fact, if good will alone could defeat our viral adversary, this pandemic would be a thing of the past based on the outpouring of love around our neighborhoods and indeed the world. Our collective determination of love and unbridled instincts of courage and compassion will continue to fortify our resolve. As Peter advises, "Cast all your anxiety on God, because God cares for you. God is with us and we are reflecting the face of the Divine to those around us, near and far."

I'll close with an epilogue from *Call the Midwife*, a fabulous PBS TV series:

> *Love is the constant by which we endure all winters and all storms; it is the climate in which all things can thrive. Welcome the darkness, embrace it as a canopy from which the stars can hang, for there are always stars when we are where we ought to be, amongst the faces we love best. Each with our place, each with our purpose, as fixed and familiar as the constellations. The darkness is beautiful, for how else can we shine?*

Shine on! Amen.

Reverend Peggy Bryan

Mount Sinai Jewish Cemetery

Walking on the footpath
beside the newly dead,
beneath sheltering
shadows of great oaks,
sorrow settles in my chest.

Come closer, gesture the trees,
with shuddering shoulders,
billows of wind buried
in their leaves.

I have come to the Jewish cemetery
to talk about death.
Cremation or burial? the advance planner
asks, sliding the brochure across the desk.

I'll take the good earth, a simple pine box,
dressed in white, barefoot, face scrubbed,
my blood intact in my veins—as I am.

When I die, I won't go up in smoke,
fallen ash, with the smell of gas
in my nostrils, the fire burning
in my lungs.

If the Messiah comes,
my spine will be whole,
my leg bones fastened, so I
can stand and walk with the ashes

of my grandmother in my arms, gathered
from the forest outside Auschwitz, fallen
beside the birch trees and on the brittle
branches of the oaks and in the cracks
where beetles burrow,

and we will go together,
not led like harnessed horses
or leashed dogs
but streaming forward like the sun
when it settles on the fields in summer.

Gail Newman

Omen

Through the scimitar shadows
by the 19th century church and graveyard,
the world is getting darker.
Crescents of light on the church walls,
slivers of hay still glowing
in a field of tiger lilies.

A morning sunset
over the ponderosa pines
and at the totality
a hush, applause, a dark feather
first light of the corona
around a dark sun.

The owl wakes up from its dream.
The Labrador quiet
at the feet of a young boy.
We traveled to this place
following a trail through time
in the footsteps of
ancient astronomers to view
a strange light.

And then that first ray of light
of the world beginning again.

Diane Frank

One Morning I Awoke in Eden

One morning I awoke in Eden.
It was obviously some mistake of Divine Justice,
     some accidental reprieve from this world of sweat and tears.
What I noticed first was the sense of timelessness,
     the feeling of eternal morning,
     as if time were standing still,
     as if my life were not ticking by,
minutes dropping into the dark well of the past, irretrievable, lost,
the future being gobbled up,
     disappearing into the ravenous mouth of my busy life.

This particular morning I awoke to
one   long   moment.
In it I noticed the curtain, not just the curtain
that had hung there for so long,
but this morning, a lacy wall of light
     that someone's hands had made,
          each lace flower spun from common thread
and from some understanding of the power of beauty
to convert the profane into the holy.
It was moving in the breeze,
moving in the buttery sunlight,
turning the oak branch outside the window into a painting.
A cardinal, chanting Matins, morning prayers,
announcing his philosophy—"I sing, therefore I am."
My body still slept, comfortable in its repose,
     languid and undisturbed
my wife abiding next to me, still asleep.
Have you ever known such peace? the grief forgotten,
     all the undone things forgiven? all debts paid?

It was just a moment, chased away by a thought,
    a remembered appointment, a list of things to do,
    the weight of life, bearing down.

It happened when I was doing nothing.
If I could only remember how to do nothing again, I would do it in a minute.
But I forget, or I never really knew how,
and it was really simply Grace,
the generosity of the present moment,
unfolding with no regard for my really important life.

Dennis Hamilton

My Face Became a Dream

My face became a dream,
and it went somewhere I don't completely understand.
The artist saw it from that angle and could not explain it to me.
The dream was about music
I could feel but not play until I left this world
and came back in another form.

The dream became a butterfly,
a prism refracting rainbows into another dimension,
a sonata flying through mysterious music.
It orbited a planet in another galaxy
and returned as the aurora borealis.

At 4:00 in the morning
an owl calls to the moon
through a sky full of fog.
Crickets hesitate.
At the edge of a dream,
just when I think I have nothing left to say,
the light starts shining.

Diane Frank

A Stranger Upon Myself

A stranger upon myself and
exiled from my soul I sit here,
listening.
Words like little waves

are washing onto
the shore of my consciousness.

I feel their cadence caress my
inner ear but understanding
gets lost in the sands
of my sorrow.

I have no bowl to hold these
aural waves.
I am longing for their meaning yet I remain
empty.

A broken vessel
lonely in the morning fog collects
drops of mist.
They cling to its cracks like heavy
pearls and drip slowly to the
bottom, and in communion
become precious
to a thirsty soul.

Ursi Barshi

Pinch the Bead Up off the Floor of the Self

Displace yourself
into the objects around you,
be the bird
making the song,
the swell of chest,
the four-note alarm,
the wheel *shushing*
over the bridge
behind you,
the low-groaned note
of the two eucalyptus rubbing.

Be less
than less than.

Every scree, cry, sigh
elongated vowel, hum,
long howl—let it
not enter you, you not
enter it—there's
no division to be rent.

Annihilate
separation, there's no ceiling,
no floor,
no you, no I, only this strung-
together bead string
of the one song
towing us all along.

David Sullivan

On the Existence of Angels

I have often considered
good thoughts to be like angels

tiny winged legions of words
pirouetting together on the tip of my pen

miniature seraphim hiding inside envelopes
between layers of scented stationery

cheery messengers, invisible cherubim
dancing single-file down telephone lines

or perhaps lingering lightly on parted lips
waiting to leap fearlessly into open air

coming to rest, at last
in the hearts of strangers and friends

Deborah Wenzler

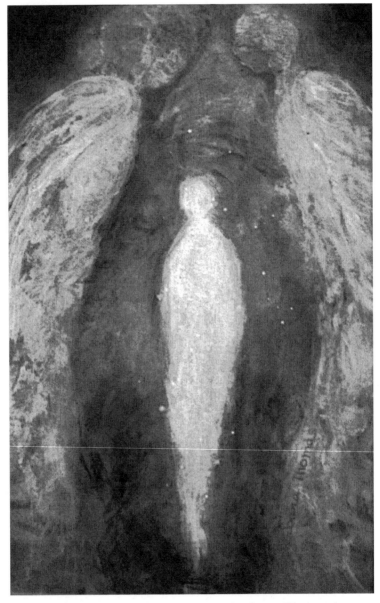

Guardian Angels–painting, Barbara Thomas

Guardian Angels

I am never alone
God has gifted to me
Two guardian angels
Who watch over me

Guardian Angels in Action

A few years ago, when I was more than 80 and not yet 90, I traveled with two of my children to Portland Oregon to attend my granddaughter's wedding. My children were happily walking together and talking, as they looked for our rental car. I gave up trying to keep up with them and walked at my own leisurely pace.

When I came to the crosswalk across four lanes of fast-moving cars, I realized I was alone; my children did not hear me when I called. They did not realize my vision was limited and in my elder years I might need assistance. I was filled with fear. There was no one around me to ask for help, simply four lanes of fast-moving cars between me and my children.

I closed my eyes and prayed, *God, help me.* Immediately I was aware of two very large spirit beings, one on each side of me. I felt so safe. The three of us stepped into the crosswalk. All cars stopped until we were on the other side of the street. The angels stayed with me until I could see my children. I was filled with amazement and gratitude, and remembered God's promise in the bible, "I will give my angels charge over thee to guide thee in all thy ways."

Barbara Thomas

What Will Save Us

We're all in this together,
looking for the songs to sing
that will hold the world together.
We might look to the soldier or scientist
to save us,
but the hero sits in silence before dawn,
looks out the window at the moon
slender and radiant in her old age,
and listens,
listens below ticking clock
and hooting owl,
listens beyond the whisper of candle flame
and the tinkle from the bells
the ants wear round their feet.
Deep in the earth,
deep in the cave of her heart,
angels sing,
and the poet transcribes.

Mary Camille Thomas

Threshold

So here we are
wishing to be plucked
from this field of uncertainty
this field of despair
by some anointed angel
Lamb of God, have mercy on us
Day after day goes by
no angel appears
not even when the bells
of the Angelus ring

But now some instinct
some painful
desire to survive
finds us at the Door
hand on knob
yearning to open it
longing to cross
the threshold—but afraid of
that which hasn't
been known before

It's much easier to be plucked
by gossamer hands
and haloed beings
so much easier
than walking on two feet
two oh-so-human feet
through the threshold
& onto blessed ground

Linda Serrato

Benediction

Bless the place where the land
Takes a sudden fall—
Bless the steady rocks that
Dream of millions of sunsets—
Bless the edge of the cliff
This cliff
Which holds death and life together
And fills me with dread.
Bless the fearless birds who
See freedom
Where I perceive certain doom.

Blessed be you who lead me
To this abyss
You, who knew this moment since
Time before time.
Gather me up into your arms
And if I must fall,
Unfold my wings.

Ursi Barshi
June 2017

Divine Whisperings–sculpture, Donna Runnalls

On Both Sides

. . . the world flows past on both sides . . . —Nazim Hikmet

What have I missed
in my rush to arrive somewhere,
to be on time – perhaps
the exquisite auburn color
of two stallions in a pasture
along the road,

or a melody in the flow
of my breaths,
the inhaling exhaling tune
of living.

I might have caught
a trace of moisture
in the rainbow-colored sphere
that slipped behind the mountain,
traveled through sunset's brilliance.

Life requests my attention
to its earthly moments,
the quickly passing splendor
by the window into nevermore.

I stop to listen
to my heartbeat,
rhythmic drumming
that counts in three-quarter time,
measures the days
I have left.

Laura Bayless

The Great River

Holly Guzman, tall and lean with curly blond hair and wireless glasses, welcomed me into her treatment room for the first time. She wore a white doctor's coat, and had been recommended to me as a master acupuncturist in town. It was three months after my sister Kathy's suicide, and I'd been unable to shake an urgent quaking fear that stole my sleep and haunted my waking moments so deeply I could barely survive the days.

"It will take time for your nervous system to heal," Holly told me. "It will be months. But I have seen this before, and I can tell you a few things about it. Right now, it seems that there is only darkness. But after a time, there will start to be a few stars. Small bits of light in the dark, easily missed. Then they'll be gone, and the dark will be all-encompassing again. You'll feel awful, and believe that you'll never be well. But then there will be a few stars again, this time a little more, and a little longer. And after a bit they will disappear again, and you'll feel awful again, and believe you've gone backwards and, again, you'll think that you'll never be well. But we'll keep doing treatments, and you will rest, and your nervous system will begin to heal. You'll start to feel your brain work again. The stars will stay longer, and you'll believe that they'll come back when they're gone. It takes a while. But healing will happen. People emerge as well as they had been before. Sometimes they come through stronger."

As she talked, I did my best to take in her words. I was softly weeping, but then, I was always weeping. I had no idea if her treatments would help or throw me off or make things worse. So many words. Did she have to talk so much? Hearing her talk, listening to anyone talk, was like fingernails against a blackboard. But somewhere what she told me landed. Holly Guzman was the one to say: *I know where you are, and I can tell you the way out.* She offered a map.

The stars did begin to appear, and they left again, and they returned. I wept my way through the fall, as if my skin had been torn off. I walked every day, sometimes twice a day in our quiet neighborhood, to release the terrible anxious energy and for something to do to fill the hours. Night after night, I sat knitting beside my wife Jean. One friend came to our house every Tuesday night and gave me a gentle massage. For months I organized my week by looking toward that nourishing evening. The stars began to burn more brightly; I could feel they were there even when I couldn't see them.

One evening in December I walked outside to take out the trash, and looked up at the night sky. Far above me, I heard the stars say, *We've got your sister, and we've got you, and you are both okay.* It was incontrovertible, and, in my state, unfettered. I took it at face value; that is to say, I took it as a real message from somewhere else. I didn't know who *we* was. I could not have imagined where the sentiment came from. But the idea crept in, and remained. Whether I could believe it, and what it would mean to live in such a universe where both my sister and I were okay, was another story entirely. But I began to contemplate it; to imagine it; to wonder.

The key was to surrender, to accept the slowness in which my nervous system could regain its own ground. It would take time; that was what Holly's map had told me. Surrender into it, do not rush. After six months, though I was hardly able to hold an ordinary conversation, I was no longer weeping through the days.

As time wore on, I tried to find reasons that I might survive when my sister had not. Finally, I came to a terrible and redeeming truth: I was not different from my sister. Not in any essential way. I was not different or set apart from her, or any suffering person, or set apart from any broken woman or man on the street, not better or healthier or exempt from shattering and unthinkable pain. I was not different from the suffering and homeless and suicides and crushed souls, who in the past I would be willing to look at but were, thankfully, separate and different from me. Well, that was undeniably over. I came to see that the wish to put myself in some other category from my sister was doomed, and, at its core, unfeeling and wrong. And then I saw something else. I would not necessarily end in my sister's tragic way, not because I was different or stronger than her. I was as wounded, tender, and fragile as any of us on this raw planet hurtling through space. The reason I might survive and heal was simply that I, like all organic beings in this world, had my own story. My sister had hers, I had mine. Both heartbroken, flawed, shattered. But our own. From that small notion, I could begin to rebuild a life.

In the end, it was the beauty and rhythms of the natural world that reclaimed my soul. I couldn't go to a lonely hermitage at the edge of the sea like the monks of my Irish heritage, but I could walk the ordinary, daily world of my neighborhood. I could jot down a few poems. I could look at the rhythmic, always-changing sky. After many months, I could begin to believe the 9th-century Irish philosopher Eirugena, who wrote that we were all part of the godhead, that the world was sacred, and furthermore we are all part of it. My much-loved sister Kathy had not been thrown to some part of creation away from the divine, and neither had I. Such a thing was not even possible. In all the terror and trauma, we were, nonetheless, both held. And in some ineffable way, we were forever healed.

The ordinary streets or my neighborhood came to be filled with the beauty that only dailiness can give, the soul of familiarity, what we see when we see a person or a place every day. How changeable things are, how the sky shifts, how our beloved is troubled one day and feeling well the next, how the terrain of the entire universe, all of life, can be seen in the journey a tree makes throughout the year, growing leaves and losing them, again and again. In dailiness, these things become large, they take on their true significance. All that had once been filling my days, from which I had been brutally wrenched, had been brushed aside as if to show me the real world, under a microscope. There were small golden wrens joyfully (there was no other word) splashing in puddles on the road after a rainy night. When the birds alighted to a branch above and the puddles quieted, morning clouds shimmered in the fresh water. Tiny raindrops settled on roses like languid diamonds. My camera began to come on walks with me, and I would lean down to capture the small and the tiny, things I would never have noticed before: mist on grasses, dried seeds and berries, light on a lemon dangling from a tree. I walked to the local creek and bowed to the living waters of the earth. The creek looked bedraggled and unkempt, but the waters running through were pure, straight from headwaters, and before that, from the sky. And before that, who knew? It was all as mysterious as my own soul, and just as sacred.

Early cartographers inscribed *Here There Be Dragons* on the out-skirts of maps to denote the unknown, terrifying parts of the land-scape. I was forced to walk through that terrain, and then I kept walking. I could feel that below or within everything was an eternal great river moving at the core of life. It fed the creek, it changed the sky, it grew the birds who played in the puddles. It was growing my heart. Things never stopped moving. In the end, what was waiting for me was the astonishing existence of morning birdsong, afternoon light flooding the violet sagebrush in our garden, the long, wide sky. It was watching the lines begin to lift from Jean's face, and kissing that face and feeling my body stir in response to hers. It was sitting down to knit in the evening, next to my beloved. The pure unadulterated joy of that honor. That I could, and did, love, that my hands moved, the good, ancient feel of the yarn. There was nowhere to discover this but in my own home, the little townhouse that became my sanctuary, Jean's garden, the ordinary roads of my neighborhood, our local creek. These places were as alive, as fully sacred, as any mountaintop or monastic temple. The great river of life led me to a place within me that had not and could not be sullied by the past.

All I had to do was wait, and simply be. The world itself was always unfolding. The great river was flowing. Creation continued. I was always and forever of it.

Carolyn Brigit Flynn
Excerpt from The Light of Ordinary Days,
forthcoming memoir/history of Ireland

Tipping Point

There comes a tipping point
when you can no longer
afford the luxury
of taking someone for granted

Maybe the point comes
after a close call
a heartbreak
a heart opening

or the sudden realization
that today's sunrise
has turned into years of sunsets streaming by
and all that can be seen in the rearview mirror
is this one precious hallowed moment

unfolding now to
reveal a crisp autumn day
of golden honey light coating every surface
warming your body
until you are sticky with the goodness of love

You breathe in
your beloved walking beside you,
inhaling the truth and beauty
the goodness
the glimmer of diamonds
sparkling thru an everyday life

and you are blinded
by the light of
awe opening to wonder
at the sheer magnitude
of mystery
You breathe it all in
the goodness filling every molecule of being

You want to hold the moment forever as it
slips away
like a happy tear sliding down the cheek
brushing your lips with
the salt and sweetness of life

and the tipping point becomes a
quickening that pierces the heart
as it travels slowly through light years
leaving the stardust of gratitude
in its wake
as we return to the light from which we came
so long ago

Jan Landry
10.14.19

−photo, Nina Koocher, Provincetown MA

Love Poem for Precarious Times

I don't think I've ever told you:
This is what makes my life worthwhile.
You.
In all your fragile quirkiness.
In all your blazing radiance.
You.
Tap-dancing down the street, sweaty, in a hurry
so serious in the seriousness of it all
trying not to breathe in the breath hovering all around you.
Or holding out your gnarly hand, your filthy fingers imploring
eyes wide and glittered with the yearning of a thousand smoky stars.
Or crying in your car, a stranger, next to mine at the stoplight
your gaze averted, your fingers tight with shame around the steering wheel.
You.
When I accidentally nudge your exquisite body and apologize
as we shuffle, eyes down, past the canned soup, the frozen peas
the sorry, bruised eggplant.
You, whom I've seen perhaps a thousand times, more,
and each time I've forgotten
to tell you I adore you
to bow, weeping, before your magnificence
to skim the soft down of your arms
to nuzzle and breathe you in as if you were the sea
a bouquet of lilacs
the first morning of snow after a long drowsy autumn.
You.
Grappling with the price of peaches
grapes from Argentina
conventional or organic.
Wondering, how much longer we may be able to have these.
You, counting out your pennies at the register.
Things are hard, no job, no stimulus check
though the government's made promises.
Your face turned away in shame.
Or your forehead, a beautiful worried twist
peeking shyly out from behind your mask

your heart so wide it's breaking
wondering if Meghan Markle is happy now
moved to LA, back with her people
white and black and every other shade of royal.
Your prayers for her, a perfect snowflake
as she and all her glorious skin shine out from the cover of *People*.
Or standing stark, six feet apart
fists high, tears streaming, marching for a hope
that humanity might finally both rise and fall to their knees
as their brothers lie bleeding, gasping right there on the sidewalk.
I just need you to know.
Even if this morning you were standing at the mirror
with your tweezers, inspecting
sneering insults to your one excellent face.
Or changing your sweater, shirt, jeans
over and over again
trying to articulate just the right look
to help you tolerate yourself and meet whatever the day might bring . . .
I couldn't live without you.
Couldn't imagine the world
a glorious field of wildflowers
each one, as precious and everyday as Dandelion
delicate and commanding as Cosmos, Impatiens,
Morning Glory, full flagrant Lily.
You, the gentle unfurling fists of fern
tight-roped high in the forest trees.
You. A perfect Rose
all thorned and finicky
petals cupped around the light of dawn,
fragrant, silent
remembering yourself: glorious heart of the Divine.

Johanna Courtleigh

Somewhere in Tibet or in my Mind

Late at night, I think about atoms and stars,
layers of infinity
reaching out to the far expanse of the universe
where there is no edge,
reaching in to the core of atoms
layer after layer
of particles, energy, light.
There is something even beyond this
which I can feel
but don't completely understand.
Somewhere, on a mountain
in India or Tibet
a monk is chanting sutras and carving *mani* stones.
He sees what I see
as a Goddess with a Thousand Arms,
and the mountain whispers her name.

Diane Frank

The Sixth Sense

Our five senses help us interact with the world we see, hear, smell, taste, or touch. But what about our sixth sense? You may say, "Sixth sense? I have only five!"

As the soul's messenger, the sixth sense bypasses the mortal mind and often appears in the guise of intuition, hunches, and conscience.

When a "premonition" turns out to be right, many people call it a coincidence. It isn't. People in primitive societies would find it hard to survive without their sixth sense. It helps them "know" where to look for water or food. It alerts them to danger. Shamans go into a meditative state to receive wisdom from unseen forces.

Everyone comes equipped with a sixth sense. What sets us apart is what we do with it. The more we notice, appreciate, and use the wisdom that comes to us through that sense, the stronger it grows and the more it can help us.

On occasion, people are born with a well-developed sixth sense, but without a solid set of values to go with it. "Fake psychics" may intuit just enough information to impress. But their motivation is not service. It's power and financial gain. True psychics' motivation to be of service allows them to be "used" by their sixth sense as channels for good.

As with everything else, we earn the right to experience the sixth sense. If we misuse or ignore it, our sixth sense will eventually go dormant. If we decide to improve our mindset by welcoming the sixth sense's valuable tips and ideas, we can reconnect. Patience is the watchword.

No matter what people today may think, reincarnation is not a sequential journey from primitive to "civilized" cultures. People can be reborn into primitive circumstances after many lifetimes in materially advanced societies. The truth is, we rise and we fall, depending on the life lessons we have yet to master. Life lessons are inner work. They are about who we are, not what we do. So the kind of society we are born into is not that important. What's key is a society that provides opportunities to grow spiritually. In its wisdom, the soul takes whatever reincarnational route is best to help us awaken.

How differently would you live your life, knowing that we are reborn many times on the spiraling wheel of life—and in different places? As black, brown, white, red, or yellow? This perspective questions some deeply held beliefs, doesn't it?

If you're looking for a sense of how real, how alive God is, you might like to try warming up your sixth sense through regular meditation. Adapt yourself to the unexpected by letting go of *doing* and settling in to *being*. Take in the guidance of your sixth sense. Breathe. Breathe in your own soul's wisdom.

Carol Kline
June 2020

Surrender

i think of beauty
the way a dry stone moistens in summer rain.
the creek bed sings! glorious smell of water on sand.
memory of a great wind slicing the mother rock.

we all become bound to one another.
lifetime after lifetime, breath upon breath
the world calls us to remember ourselves.

kiss your lover's hand, the earth taste of her
rich sweet holy

love begins here, in a fistful of dirt
flung toward the future.
familiar form
bone muscle flesh

a body waits for a body.
at the edge of the clouds,
unseen lives think themselves into our dreams—
voice heard upon waking,
swirling colors in the dark,
the self that is ever-present.

this we choose to know,
like the way we choose to know
how water hits a solid thing
between your eyes
light is born!

the universe surrenders Itself for you
oh, great chorus of god!
there is no silence
behind the silence
you do not hear.

listen . . .

Karen Bartholomew

The Fourth Winter of Solitude

It was the fourth winter I had spent in ancient caves of the underworld.
The damp, cold sweat of tree roots, moist acrid smell of decay in
the depths of the forests of my inner travels were familiar territory.

I was lost, the familiar trails worn away by time now;
smooth, trackless, leading nowhere
that was ever before a somewhere.

Awaiting the harbinger that emerges from the other side of dawn,
great wings wrapping me in feathery folds of blissful forgetfulness . . .
before the change arrives.
The past is irretrievable, shrouded in smoky haze, drowned in oceans of tears…
before the shift arrives.

The future weaves, lurching forward,
a ribbon of golden dust leading downward,
a sorrowful eye; a hopeful eye, each peering through opposing windows,
one beaming inwards into memory while the other searches without
into a future still only possibility.

Somewhere, somehow…
I am as yet caught in an in-between, not yet released into an apex of insight.

Curiosity beckons me forward around a bend in the road,
there is a splendor not imaginable before midnight.

Now stars graze the fraying edges of she who I once inhabited,
sprinkling cobwebs of despair with bubbling laughter.
They wink at my stubborn will and point to a milky road
that streams across the skies.

New meaning is unwritten yet...
I have long grown used to tossing the cards high in the crystalline air
and reading meaning as they fall, strewn on deserted ground.

Perhaps, meaning is of no import in these times of depthless depth
   and vast dimension,
light and shadow, now less distinct than ever before history could
   remember . . .

Remembering to forget the past,
a blur of incidents and incidentals . . .
yet, holding lightly this sprinkling of stardust that is
a trusting in matrix and memory and mother
yet preserving the faith in wisdom and truth and father.
Love persists still, hidden behind veils of Silence.

Eva Rider

Third Wind

What sustains me? I draw a card: *Three of Wind: Recognition.*
Metamorphosis. Transformation. Transmutation. Having Become.

~

The Last Instar. I remember: I hatched from an egg. I ate greens. I
grew. There were so many times I was afraid. In my second instar,
before the second shedding, I was in a state of despair, fear, anger. I
looked around my world: all I could see was predation. Organized
violence. War. I cut thousands of black armbands and passed them
out at demonstrations. *No More War.* At the end of the second
instar, I discovered Tarot. Tarot became my counselor, my friend, my
companion. She was also a way to access my innermost soul. She was
the medium that led me to You, You who cross the dimensions to
speak to me. Thank you, Beloved. Thank you.

The Chrysalis. I shed my skin for the last time. In the final hours
of the darkest time, in the final hours, when all the world seemed so
confining, I felt I would either burst into a pile of guts or explode into a
supernova. Then, the *magic* happened. I had already been through five
instars, each one more challenging than the one before. As I got bigger,
my challenges got bigger. I had lost my friend. I was surrounded by
illness and death. The world seemed to be collapsing as never before.
Even though fifty wars raged across the planet, war was only part of it.
Now, I could see so clearly the damage the human species had done:
ecocide, genocide, matricide, fratricide, homicide. I found myself
hanging upside down on the end of a branch—by my last pair of feet.
I was conflicted. I wanted to drop, to fall, to jump. I wanted to take
the pill and end it all, and yet I could not release. Immobilized, then,
I entered a deep state of meditation. In time—out of time—my head,
which had been hanging down, began to sway. My head swayed this
way and that, moving until it hit the branch—thought ceased—and the
whirling began.

The Meltdown. I had a head once, but then it was gone. My legs,
tight skin, guts—all disappeared. No more thought. No more war.

The Imaginal Cells. Green, then blue, then orange and black,
squished. No thought. Only sensation. The self of me—no self—again
pushing. *Pura vida.*

The Emergence. Thin encasement splits. Gasping. Grasping.

The Wet Wings. These appendages. This scaly body. Wires coming out of my head. *Where am I? Who am I?* Wait. *Wait!* I can *see!* Oh, Beauty. Can you hear the purple flowers singing? The Glory steels my breath. Oh! I *breathe!* Oh! *Electric magic streaming. Pulsing. Swelling. Pumping.* I become *gigantic.*

In the End, there is Sight, there is Flight, there is Majesty.

Next Card: Mastery.

~

In the end, *Tarot of the Spirit* has sustained me for three and a half decades. Deathing and Birthing have become one movement. Faith is the lesson.

Pamela Eakins

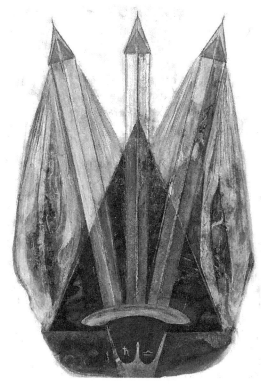

Three of Wind: Recognition–painting,
Joyce Eakins, *Tarot of the Spirit*

untitled

"Away from your
remaining
chained
boxed
trapped artifices
of preconditioned centuries-old
conquer and dominate

Away

Look up to the sky
look out to your furthest inner ring of life
and expand
past the comfort of delusion

shattering and slingshotting into forms of pure light

nothing else
on a plateau
of focused green grass
steady in the unforgiving wind
holding your hand while getting out of your skin
and into consciousness

shattering and slingshotting into forms of pure light"

said the essence of living, to me,
meandering with the red-winged blackbird
and reverberations
of countless miles
in the unknown
crashing,

like waves
like stars
like anger becoming akin
to soft stones in a river.

Terese Garcia

Floating in the Sky

Everything's a middle ground, a piece of sorrow floating in the sky.

You catch it and bring it in close. Bring it to your lips, or maybe it's your heart. You reach out your hand. You don't even have to try. It's all happening automatically. As everything does.

That's what the guru in India said. One of the major cosmic truths, and who are you to say he's wrong? Who are you to say anything at all? When you were warned, over and over again, that there was no one really there at all.

There, on the train, waiting to come into the station. There, in line at the bus stop. If it was a dream, maybe yours, maybe someone else's. What is the self you claim as "me," anyway? If we are all One. Another cosmic truth he kept repeating. "There is thinking but no thinker. There is doing but no doer. There is listening, but no listener. There is no person there at all."

You, at the top of the temple, looking out at that vast expanse of sky. All those scrawny Indian trees below. The air thick as mud, thick as night, heavy with the wind of things, blowing gently. You can almost see it as the trees sway like a drone-y melody. A field of dragon flies lifting and darting, as if the whole world was magic. "Everything is happening automatically." And maybe even you, swatting away a mosquito. *Be a Buddha*, you whisper silently. A blessing, as you kill that sucker and the blood begins to rise and the poison it inflicted into your sticky skin calls to your hand and your nails dig in, "flesh of my flesh," and you have now become God, the Lord giveth and the Lord taketh away.

And then, perhaps, a smoky moon, as all Indian moons must be. And you wonder, *why* this land of beauty and chaos, of grace and grief? Millions of children, filthy in their ratty beds, their hollow bellies growling a lullaby.

You watch the night taking wing as bats begin to dive, and here you are, again, India, home of your soul. Flies in the eyes and gods on every corner. In this vast unfolding of light that is the world.

You repeat, "It's all perfect," even as you sit complaining about the food, the heat, how you didn't sleep last night, those damn mosquitoes, and why is the streetlight so frigging bright just outside the room?

Someone comes with tea. Someone bows their head. Someone mops the floors and makes the beds, and, curious, rummages through your things, carefully, never having seen quite so much stuff—*you know Westerners!*—as they giggle and gossip in a language you'll never understand.

But those eyes. How deep they go. How present and beautiful. Even, or especially, the kids. Their wide faces, their beautiful smiles, every tooth a jewel, gleaming. Even the ones on the street corner for the day, dirty hands outstretched, their ratty clothes barely covering them properly. India. A magnificent Disneyland ride, and you, getting to watch it all from the safety and comfort of your air-conditioned taxi, this foreigner, everyone's curious, peeking in as they rickshaw by.

You smile or look away. Depending. If it's the wide-eyed one, or the one with the clouds encroaching. You can see it all right there. The guy, sinister on his motorcycle, probably some kind of overlord. Or the family of five, squished onto one seat, scarves flying, celebratory.

It's all good because, caring though you may be about human suffering and everything else wrong with the world, you, after a day of shopping and seeing what there is to be seen—pity the poor beggars, the suffering ones out there on the rubbled sidewalks, especially the old women for whom you become a hero and a saint, tossing a few rupees down, careful not to touch, who knows what kind of illness they might carry, like a mangy dog, and that one there, bringing her hand over and over to her mouth to let you know she's hungry—you've tossed down the equivalent of what, a dime, a quarter?, and you are suddenly her best friend and she, all toothless smiles and runny eyes, doesn't know she'll become a story of your generosity as you rumba back over the potholed streets, back to hot water and a good bed and room service, maybe with dessert and wine tonight.

Yes, life is good. And when it's time—you are traveling business class, thank God—you'll get your groggy self to the airport at one or two a.m. (the flight's so early!), wait in the business class lounge, and finally get to lie down when you get on board. They will offer you champagne first thing, lucky sod, and you'll settle on in, in your own little cubby. Recline and doze and drift, watching movie after movie on your own personal screen, while they bring you another hot toddy because your throat's a little raw from all that pollution.

And, because everything is happening automatically, you'll find yourself, miracle of miracles, in a completely different world just a few inconvenient hours from the departure gate. A limousine driver with a sign will hold up your name—important, significant you!—and take you to your next hotel. "There is traveling but no traveler." And you are in another world! Far from the smoky night, the incessant honking and people milling the streets at three, four, five a.m. "What are they doing?!" you might ask your driver, but he doesn't speak English, and even if he did, you would never understand that there is doing but no doer. That they are simply being. That this is their life, perhaps arduous, but still. Holding down the night, as the wild dogs ruffle the garbage, and Brahmin cows dream, and the temple boys scrub the smooth soft marble, mumbling their prayers, keeping the whole world turning.

Johanna Courtleigh

Delete, Delete

Please don't bother reading this
instead
delete, delete, delete

My inbox is full of recycled wisdom
words of inspiration from
great teachers with pithy insights
Tara, Jack, Joseph, Sharon,
and then Sharon again

Oh and don't forget Jon, Dan, Rick and Rhonda
I love them all,
I feel like I know them on a first-name basis
They send me daily emails
even Ram Das, who died last December, is on the circuit
reminding me to be here now

I scroll through my in-box
like a hungry ghost
window shopping,
every day a plethora of offerings, podcasts
guided meditations, wisdom teachings,
and one mindfulness summit after another
with the same cast of characters
including Sharon
I sign up for them all and don't listen to any of them
delete, delete delete

Recycled wisdom
from recycled wisdom
all good, but...

Still I scroll and scroll
there is no satisfying this hungry ghost
who eats but is not nourished,
whose sadness cannot be soothed
whose broken heart
no dharma angioplasty can fix

I roam and rummage
through the basement of my consciousness
with the glazed hollowed look of one who is lost,
gone, disconnected from themselves and others
not tethered to the here and now, but far far away

Not gone as in *Gate, Gate, Paragate**
no this is a different kind of gone,
of someone who looks but doesn't see
touches but doesn't feel
what is right there in the center of my heart
a burning flame
a longing for freedom
that comes from a place that is already free

and the longing is nothing more
than love returning to itself
feeding on the fresh immediacy of truth
emerging
moment to moment
and devouring
the layers of separation
the hungry ghost feasts on her own nectar
and becomes a vast transparent expanse
that is nowhere and everywhere
Paragate, Parasamgate*
gone to the furthest shore

Delete delete delete

Jan Landry
5.22.2020

*From the Buddhist *Heart Sutra*, translated "Gone, gone beyond,
gone utterly beyond"

God throws me down,

hard dice clacking back alley concrete;
god seals me in a plastic tube
and sends me down a pneumatic chute
like a police precinct's confiscated porno mag;
god kneads my flesh with pulpy fists;
god shows me how to hold my lips
while she applies lipstick,
puckering her own to show me how;
she sits beside me during driver's ed,
her foot hovering above the extra brake;
it sings this morning's song in the shape
of a magpie, then cross-rubs its beak
on the branch it perches on; god
is at the end of every staticky dropped connection;
god paints the white borders of the end zone;
sculpts the papaya-shaped coffin
out of soft wood, then paints it stroke by stroke;
she hands me the 3/8ths Phillips screwdriver
when I wheel out from under the Buick's chassis;
refills my chamomile tea without interrupting
my confession; god's the one selling inner tubes
by the rushing river current, cheap;
puts in the rope swing forty feet up
on the tree that leans out over the Connecticut;
smiles while he spoons succotash
onto my tray in the homeless shelter food line;
suspends the Nikes on a telephone wire
when the coins of my sole's holes grow too large;
every coincidence isn't; god lays his—her—its—thumb
on the scale, or whatever god holds that kind of weight
whispers: *There's more to be done, get on with it.*

David Sullivan

ART from
CHAOS

La Loba is a mythical wild woman, a gatherer of bones. Once found and pieced back together, creatures of the natural world become whole again. Renewed, they are given a second wind. The spirit of La Loba is alive in those I admire: our healers, believers, artists and truth seekers. Her prayer is one of perseverance, bringing hope and strength to all who suffer. -BA

La Loba's Prayer–Beth Appleton
Cut paper digital assemblage

Art from Chaos
The Goddess at the Crossroads

In the present disorienting moment, as we find ourselves more physically isolated and anxious, we have an increased need to communicate our shared experience of disruption and our vision of the road ahead. Making art is an intentional response to forces we cannot control; our creations declare that our choices do matter, both for good and ill. Art that is shared in public places invites us to pause, remember, and imagine what it means to be human beings in community, especially when humanity and community are threatened.

Now, in this time of quarantine, I initiated a project called Art from Chaos to invite people in my community and beyond to create their own art installations near home and visible to passersby. These offerings give us a creative connection and remind us of our essential need for each other. An Art from Chaos Facebook page makes it possible for us to share and respond to the art we have made.

For my offering, I was moved to create "the goddess at the fork in the road." In ancient Greece she was known as Hecate, the goddess of crossroads and thresholds. The figure of the goddess was constructed largely of found materials: a gourd for her head, a skirt made of magnolia leaves, arms of branches and hands of twisted wood. I installed her at a crossroads in my neighborhood, and at her base I placed a scroll of tree bark on which was written a message attributed to the goddess.

Behind—
Contemplate where you have been.
Before you—
Consider where the path you choose
will lead you.
Your choices, large and small
shape the world.

I introduced Hecate to my neighbors one evening in May. It was a festive event with music and a sense of celebratory pride in our community. My hope was that she will spark others to make art from chaos, for the good of all.

Norine Cardea

At the Crossroads–photo, Hali Tauxe

Dialogue with the Goddess

During my daily morning walks in the neighborhood, I passed Hecate rising like a ship's figurehead at the crossroad, her gnarly fingers pointing in opposite directions. Hecate's traditional abode is the underworld, but Norine's inspiration summoned a local visitation. The goddess was as stern and implacable as an ancient oracle, and her urgent message demanded a response: *Pause, Consider, Choose.*

I was moved to dialogue with her in a poem painted on a blue signboard, which I placed beside her as an interpretive offering. Like the goddess, the poem is wild and improbable—art from chaos, making a way out of no way.

Marda Messick

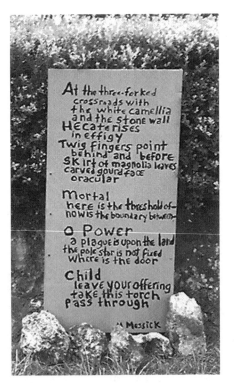

top: Hecate at the Threshold–photo, Susan Cerulean
below: Hecate's Message–photo, Hali Tauxe

−sculpture, Nora Sarkissian

What the Muse Said

Become a poet. Live it.
Become the old one
with notebook and pen,
the wordsmith by the lake
counting swans.
See the geese rise. See the world.
See. Only your eyes can do this.
Everything hinges on this:
the lives of all you love
lie now in the cusp of your pen.
Do it for them.
Become someone else,
someone serious with the world.
Take your book, read,
and go outside. Your feet
will tell you poems
but only if you are walking.
Slough off the last doubts
like an uplifting swan
shuffling the waters from white feathers.
Fly. Push off,
though it is ancient to you,
and sometimes foreign
and strange. Make your home
in the sky, and follow
the letters to a new day
you sense waiting,
the one beyond words,
past language, but
able to be found among them, even so.

Carolyn Brigit Flynn

And if I Don't Write?

One morning when I was at my desk, the words kept rebuffing me. Not one that touched the paper was even close to what I wanted to say, and doubt gnawed at me as though I were its bone. "It's not like you're getting paid to be here," I said to myself, "so don't write."

I walked away from my notebook feeling much relieves—I really didn't have to write, now did I? I took a deep breath and thought about what I'd do with the suddenly open hours. Until the impulse to write called me back. Apparently, it was going to be one of those days—damned if I did and damned if I didn't. Pushed to the edge, I relinquished control.

When I returned to the desk, here's what came:

If I don't write, I won't die. My eyes will still see what they see, this heart, too. Blood won't stop its pulse-work. Feet won't forget the forest is for wandering through. Nor will I be less inclined to comment on the world's beauty.

If I don't write, my imagination won't stop its daily moment-by-moment insistence, not to make something out of nothing, but to make a frog from a prince, a window out of a wall, a day out of despair.

Without a pen in hand, ,a poem in mind, phrases turned over in mind, my imagination won't   harden into the gray, flat matter of reason. I won't forget to proclaim. Still, I'll be a diviner.

Or will I?

If I don't write, will I lose my way, give up my song, forgetting its value—speech that for years I begged for, clumsily stuttered toward, then thrust my way into, and occasionally found waiting at my doorstep, ready? If I don't write, will my imagination atrophy and, like an unused limb, dry up and wither? Will a hard shell form around my ribcage, a gnarled claw overtake my pen-holding hand?

Yes. If I don't write, my eyes will become veiled and darkly hooded. Scales will bend my back. My tongue will thicken into a knot that not even the nimblest sailor will be able to untie.

And what if *you* don't write?

Patrice Vecchione
Excerpt from My Shouting, Shattered, Whispering Voice

Life is Good–drawing, Sarojani Rohan

Smudge

"Bəru-n became my spirit guide. Acij will do that to you," Ming Lee recollected, her deft hands assessing the twin gashes on Bird's back. Inga laughed, a dry cackle, knowing all too well the truth in that statement. She wobbled to the far end of the room to refill the kettle, old bones creaking with each step.

"Tea, anyone?" she called out behind her, knowing already their answers. Bird, of course, would take whatever given and down it with a smile. Ming Lee, on the other hand, engrossed in her work and far too tuned in to her ancestors (at least Inga thought as much), wouldn't have any of it. Inga laughed to herself, how different those two could be.

The cuts were growing, deepening. Ming Lee made a salve from Inga's herb garden just outside: mugwort for divine guidance, pennyroyal for protection, a bit of yarrow. Gotu kola for expansion. Snakeskin for release. She made the brew on the summer solstice and let it absorb lunar energy for three cycles, as the scabs on Bird's back began to form. Different than what her grandmother had made for her, all those years ago, but although the ingredients had changed the old magic still ran strong.

Bird tried not to squirm, the ointment cold and soothing on the throbbing cuts between her shoulder blades. Instead, she took to focusing on the story, though she'd heard it all before. The thumb, the tree, the voices. The pseudo-shamanic journey of her elders. To be sure, she wanted nothing more than to sit and daydream and feel the inhale exhale flow of the moment; the stories of old held little interest to her, despite how invested in them Ming Lee seemed to be.

Bird flinched as Ming brushed a particularly tender spot.

"They're growing in strong," Ming Lee said, eyeing the baby feathers, red and heavy, already emerging from the slits. Inga came over, bringing a steaming mug to Bird. Her pungent smell startled Ming Lee and for a second there was only one girl before Inga, and not two. Just as fast, they split again, and Inga let out a hefty groan.

"They're growing in *painful*, is what they're doing," Bird chimed in, laughing it off with a shake of her head, smiling. When the old woman gave her the mug, Bird tried to sniff out the ingredients: rosemary, reishi, maybe even some reindeer piss? And tincture. Definitely tincture. Bird giggled again and took a sip, relaxing into the aches in her back.

Inga sighed, watching the two girls. It was one thing dealing with the intuitions of the would-be *babaylan*, or the rose-tinted musings of the young crystal child — but to bring them together, to have them remember? She sighed, taking a gulp from her mug. She knew she had to help, but the task was a hard one, and she was ready to retire from all these seraphic duties. *Soon*, she reminded herself. *They'll wake up soon.*

Cassidy Parong

Callas Art Quilt, Emergence Quilt–Mary Kay Hamilton

Quilting

Since sheltering in place, my husband and I have become more domesticated. Our normal busy social life of retirement is on hold, as are all our travel plans. Dennis is baking more breads, pies, cookies, scones, etc. and playing music on his guitar and mandolin. We both pay much more attention to our yard and gardens. I probably don't do more cleaning, though it seems I change the sheets on our bed more often; maybe because I spend more time there than before.

What I have done much more of, however, is quilting, an expensive habit I picked up a couple of years into retirement. I believe I enjoyed shopping for fabric and poring over quilting magazines more than producing finished products. But now, I delve into the extensive stash of fabric I have accumulated over these last few years. Surprisingly, I can spend several hours a day playing with my fabrics, cutting and sewing.

I have made an alarming number of quilts: bed quilts, lap quilts, art quilts. I start planning the next one before I've finished the current one. It is keeping me sane.

Never having thought of myself as an artist, I find solace in creating art. I play with colors and shapes, realistic scenes or still life, and abstracts; nothing is off the table. I have become appreciative of having this time to stay at home and hum along in my sewing room till the sun sets. I keep my hands busy while watching or listening to the grim news on TV or radio, or on good days, the live music drifting down the stairs from husband's playing (accompanied by the aromas from his oven).

I don't know what I would be doing otherwise, staying at home like this. I still miss my friends and family time and my community involvement. But I have something to look forward to every day if I choose. It keeps me from climbing the walls—especially because my walls are now covered with quilts.

Mary Kay Hamilton

The World is on Fire

I enjoy the challenge of creating a soup. A truly good soup is an acknowledgement you've arrived as a "skillful cook." As any cook and most eaters know, to make a nourishing, delicious soup is an art. Good soup elicits a yum. Soup cannot be rushed. Making soup takes time, time and patience. Time, patience and lots of mistakes helped with salt, hot sauce, perhaps even the trusty cover-up of heaps of grated cheese.

To begin, it is essential to slowly layer, with respect, prepared ingredient by ingredient, by ingredient. Sauté until caramelized just so, to bring out the sweetness from within. Thoughtful consideration with a plan is called for, allowing for creative adjustments. Spices of course are required. Add individual spices, unique in color, smell, from around the world, your backyard, then allow to mingle in community over time. Simmering and time brings out depth of flavor and richness of taste.

Adjust the fire just so. Rushing the process with too high a flame can cause boiling over and ruin your soup. With impatience, you'll end up with a watery, uninteresting soup that requires drastic outside help, or the compost heap.

This reminds me of one of my favorite Rumi poems, "Chickpea to Cook."

> A chickpea leaps almost over the rim of the pot
> where it's being boiled.
>
> 'Why are you doing this to me?'
>
> The cook knocks him down with the ladle.
>
> 'Don't you try to jump out.
> You think I'm torturing you.
> I'm giving you flavor.'

The world is on fire and we're burning in the cauldron of anger, hatred, confusion, fear. The world is on fire and we're burning in the cauldron of truth, hope, love. Humanity is cooking. We're on fire and we're burning in the cauldron. We are in a collective soup, swimming around, half asleep, bumping into each other, pushing away, coming together, struggling to define the who, why, what. How to make sense of the senseless? When enough is enough and there is no recipe to go on, we explode, implode and fall in towards each other. We are swirling in a soup of our glorious humanity: ugly, beautiful, plain, broken. What is this soup we are making? The outcome is a mystery.

We're being cooked into our humanity. No matter what anyone may think, no one can be left out. We share this spinning blue-green earth. We are an abundant harvest of amazing bounty from across this nation: up and down, rural, urban, beachside, along mighty rivers, under great trees, in broken tenements, over and under bridges, in dry desert, reservations, suburbs, university towns, old towns, abandoned towns, crowded into apartments, ghettos of despair or mansions of ridiculous privilege. Unique, splendid, robust. Each and every one essential to add just the right taste, depth, texture to awaken the palate. To create an aromatic swoon to tickle your nose. Wake all your senses. A unique soup of remarkable flavor, like no other. Bursting with robust daring, overtones of courage, with a back note of melancholy joy and nuances of tender-hearted love.

Come sit at the table. It's plain but it is strong. Hold out your begging bowl. I will ladle in soup of such unique flavor that you will break into song, halleluiah, blessed be, praises be to the goddess. I am now your teacher. I once was your student. I bow in reference to the unknowable. Deep bow in reverence, head to earth, body in prayer. May goodness rise to the surface.

Carolyn Davis Rudolph

Envisioning

1.

Nothing behaves anymore. Lines are no longer interested in the shortest distance between two points; instead they meander like a slow-moving stream. This distortion is the beginning stage of macular degeneration. For me, it's almost as hard to imagine not seeing clearly as it is to imagine not being. As if I might disappear bit by bit as my vision diminishes.

My anxiety runs wild. My retinal specialist says there is little that can be done. I can't accept the finality of this prognosis. I diligently research alternative treatments, making radical changes in my diet while a variety of vitamins and supplements accumulate on my counter. Then the big discovery: an acupuncture clinic in New Jersey that specializes in eye conditions. It's 3000 miles from my home in California, but I make a leap of faith and sign up for two weeks of treatment the following month. Taking action calms my anxiety. Now I need to dive deeper.

I decide to make a mosaic. I sit on the flour, surrounded by stones, beads, jewelry pieces. Without hesitation, I reach for two medallions— one with an oak tree image and the other a spiral design—and place them a short distance from each other. As I surround each medallion with a ring of white stones, they suddenly become eyes. I wind a turquoise necklace in a horizontal figure-eight infinity loop around the two "eyeballs," then place one more row of white stones around the turquoise.

I am stunned by the effect of these simple placements. Each circle highlights the adjacent one, becoming two miniature mandalas. I intuit that the turquoise stones are healing, as if their water-like color soothes my eyes and plumps the retinal cells.

This reminds me of *The Anthropology of Turquoise* by Ellen Meloy. I pull her book from the shelf and flip to the last page. These words reverberate:

> I would keep my turquoise, not trade it for anything. It is the stone that strengthens the eyes, said the Persians, the desert dweller's equivalent of the bulletproof vest against pain or demonic influences. It is water, say the Zuni. For the Aztecs

this is the color that supplies the heart. For me, it is simply instinct, and perhaps this is all that a person can try to put into each of her days: attention to the radiance, a rise to the full chase of beauty.

Turquoise, the stone that strengthens the eyes and protects. My instinct somehow knew this old teaching. Turquoise, the color that feeds the heart. Of course, without heart there is no healing. Turquoise, a stone of mystery and paradox: rigid and hard yet evoking the fluidity of tropical waters. Facing a diagnosis that can seem unmovable as a boulder, I now imagine aqua water enveloping the obstructive retinal deposits, loosening their grip.

When I return to my mosaic, it no longer appears two-dimensional. The oak branches stretch out toward me, the twisting roots search in every direction, the spiral expands. And the turquoise strand is no longer stuck in a static figure eight. Instead, I see it rotating around its center point, reaching into radiance. Hope stirs for healing beyond what eye charts can measure.

2.

I read this story to my writing group and rebuild the mosaic sculpture on the coffee table. I share that the medallions relate to each of my dead parents. An oak tree image was embossed on my mother's gravestone, inspired by a beloved tree that sheltered our family home. The silver spiral was a gift from my father, an exact replication of his innovative antenna design, a symbol of transmission and reception.

My friends are moved by my peril and my efforts and want to help. They suggest a ritual to prepare me for my upcoming acupuncture clinic. I gratefully surrender.

Our teacher gets her drum. A candle is lit. The drumbeat starts steady as a heartbeat. I lie on the floor and close my eyes. A soft pillow is gently placed beneath my head. The repetitive drumbeat provides a trancelike thread while my friends begin to transfer the mosaic to my face. One places the oak medallion on my right eye and the spiral on my left. I feel the cool weight of each on my eyelids, immediately comforted by this contact. As another encircles my eyes with the turquoise figure eight, I experience fluid energy moving through the string of stones. I sense the flutter of hands as the white stones are creatively placed around my head. Another woman begins to slowly weave her body in movement as sinuous as the oak branches and spiral.

I am transported: by the ancient practice of drumming, the connection to my ancestors, the touch of stones and the tending of loving hands. For most of my life I have been a dedicated introvert, looking for strength and spiritual guidance from within, not unlike the roots of the oak seeking sustenance below the earth's surface. But life keeps teaching. Trees flourish in community, communicating and sharing nutrients through their intertwining root systems. Oak branches reach out beyond the trunk as the signal-seeking spiral circles outward. I am learning that healing does not need to be solitary.

The drumbeat begins to slow, becoming softer and softer. Movements cease, quiet gathers around us. My entire being sings as I feel the presence of radiance and our rise to the full chase of beauty.

Marilyn DuHamel

–photo, Marilyn DuHamel

Dancing in the Park after Sheltering in Place

Beneath the canopy of a maple tree
we ladies twirl our skirts, ballerinas
trapped in a little girl's music box
unopened for three months
newly released
we turn in mirror memory
lovely pink tutu prima ballerina
purple crepe ballgown belle of the evening
we dance to a trio harmonizing Beatles songs
All the Lonely People
unfrozen we step from a Degas painting
brushstroke skin of our limbs
giddy with new found freedom
complete the arabesque began last century
in the grace of our shadows silhouette
another era please
innocent, naive, elegant
Here Comes the Sun
out of our caves
we dance in a tribal circle
dance the dance from the beginning of time
the shadow of maple leaves tattooing our faces
out of our minds
Lucy in the Skyyyy
our skirts shape the lines of our hips
furl at our ankles
we pound out a flamenco crescendo
with Diiiiiiamonds
undulate a belly dance from hips through fingertips
our undyed hair silvering
under a day moon sky.

Joanna Martin

The Genie

The dancing girl in the yellow silk pants
shimmered in my dream.
She was a flame that kept burning in the morning.
If I bring her to Aladdin,
I can gaze into her chocolate eyes
and lose myself in the maze of her footsteps.

Aladdin thinks I am his servant,
but every morning I weave a dream
into the world where he walks by the river.

I hold my prism in the river of sunlight,
each wave of color a possibility
to weave footsteps into the world
I paint every morning.
I can dream or disappear
into the longing for the light
that becomes invisible
inside the bronze of my lamp.

Every morning, you choose
to dance or disappear.

Diane Frank

love is all there is—watercolor, d'vorah darvie

Duet–Jory Post, Santa Cruz, CA

The SOCIETY
of PLAYFUL
SPIRITS

–photo, Nina Koocher, Paris France

Love Pandemic

Last night I had a dream that I was touched by an angel and became infected with unconditional love that I could pass to others by hugging, touching or kissing and then they, too, would infect others with the love pandemic.

The first person I infected was my wife, Joanna, then together we started to infect all of our family and friends. It was contagious to the core of our souls. First we hit Capitola, all the places we go dancing: the Sand Bar, Zelda's and Paradise Grill. We hugged and kissed all our friends and also everyone we met. We stopped at St. Joseph's Church for Friday Lenten fish fry dinner, infected everyone we came in contact with, and later infected shoppers along the Pacific Garden Mall and people who worked at El Palomar restaurant. On our way to the Santa Cruz library, we encountered some homeless people asking for change. We gave them some money, but more importantly, we gave them our love virus. It made them smile and feel good inside, reminding us that homeless people still feel love inside their hearts. Our love virus started to spread like wildfire all over Santa Cruz County, then all over California and all through the United States of America.

Soon the whole world was infected with the love virus. For the first time in human history there really was peace on earth. One planet living as one. No more war, no more hate, only forgiveness and love to share. May we never recover from the love pandemic.

Lalo Alvarez

COVID Coiffure

After months of sheltering in place,
hair salons shuttered,
my manicured coif loses shape,
reverts to lengthening plaits
of white, silver, gold.

My husband's bald spot enlarges.
To distract the eye
from thinning scalp fringe,
straggling gray wisps
approaching his shoulders,
he cultivates a snowy goatee.

As shutdown persists,
civil unrest escalates,
democracy falters.
During viral déjà vu,
we relive the turbulent sixties,
morph into straggly-haired hippies.

Jennifer Lagier

The Girl Who Could Twirl in the Swirl of Life
with All its Many-Headed, Hidden and Forbidden Obstacles, and Her Companion, the Wolf

In the Beginning…

The Girl… which Girl…this Girl, among many girls out there, wandered the streets of indiscreet disclosures and idiosyncrasies, becoming more and more of an anomaly by the hour, until she found herself looking into the eyes of the fiercest wolf she had ever seen—well really the only wolf, as girls are not often acquainted with wolves, at least some girls.

It was of course no disgrace, as complex as things had been, with shoes flying through the air and tomato soup cans lingering in the shadows of others' hindsight. For if we had foresight, things wouldn't get so out of control. We were all sure of that, at least, as we shall see things from the beginning and possibly to the end. But then what is the end, my friend, but finding a way not to pretend that shoes fit when they don't?

So the Girl among many girls went for a walk, the last walk around the block. Meanwhile the ones in so-called authority tied strings of resistant unsubstantial filings, like stones, to an apron of their choosing.

Especially when making capricious stew, you might lose your freedom to choose.

The Girl Walks Between Two Worlds

The Girl who could twirl and whirl in life's little swirls was walking between two worlds one day on a tightrope between the bondage of should be this, should be that, if you want to be free, ask a cat. Finding herself at the edge of the forest between a cement world and one more vibrant and green, she fell in through a crack, headlong. Floating her way between seasons and reasons, between sparks of light and shades of ubiquitous turnips, turning up everywhere, landing into a lush, soft, welcoming moss; and just like that, there she went, from one life to another.

Sometimes you just get lucky enough to fall through the cracks (imagine that), insisted the cat, smiling.

Entering the Forest of Dreams

With a thud a rumble and a tumble, she awoke to find herself in the forest of dreams, her wounds being licked clean by the wolf, all the salty wounds of a lifetime, hearing faint cries and screams from a time she could hardly remember.

She came to, with the shaking of her head. Memories from the time filled with dread shook off and fell like darkened pebbles into a new stream.

As we all live on the edge of the forest . . .

> between pleasure and hypocrisy
>
> between a sandstorm and a morass
>
> between you and me
>
> between serene green moss and a loud screeching
>   in the soul.

Me, I'm not so sure, so I just keep doing what I do and hope for a break in the cosmic weather.

Or better yet, a complete cosmic makeover.

Nora Sarkissian

–painting, Nora Sarkissian

18

On our weekly walk a friend tells me she wants
to have more commas in her life. It takes me half a
beat before I understand what she is saying; before
I laugh; before I say, "good for you," her life often
like a run-on sentence that leaves the reader breathless
until thirty-six pages later a period brings to a close
a wondrous exuberance.

I've always loved the dash, but lately I am drawn to
semicolons, which meet a different kind of need;
they offer a longer pause. They also appeal to my
residual Canadianism; a bit more formal, they
step in and bring order to my fractured life while
remaining open to moments before and after.

Sometimes these days, I catch myself not breathing;
as if I could protect myself from life's horrors by not
inhaling; as if a period could save me; or brackets; or
a blank page. This is not what is meant by learning to
be still.

Lauren Crux
excerpt from "Little Rambles"

On the Object of Being Snarled

(i) Spin Cycle: An Unraveling

Teeth brandishing, lips pulled back: smile. The quickest way of building qi. I see through your teeth transparent. The translucent glimmer of that snag-tooth. *Don't turn away.* Come child, we're only beginning.

(ii) Rinse Sequence

Pisces. Overemotional and overwhelmed. It only took one time for me to read that and Nope, out. Better to look towards the east, where at least I'm a rat. A *fire* rat, to be sure, because even then I knew my element was not the fickle licks of water.

In the west, I'm the last. The east: the onset. Following Helios's arch, I suppose: there and back again, round and round the prickly pear — my little rat wheel of entanglement. Set to perpetual motion in the alignment game (so close, just a little furthur![1]) always coming and going, like the wanderings of closet men[2] (how are they never sad?), and coming again. Always in the process of becoming. *Be patient, my child, and respect the cycles.* The start. The finish. The superpositioning thereof.

(iii) Tumble Dry

It seems that I'm caught on this wheel of fate[3] waiting for the spoke gaps to expand into ether. Waiting for the ether to bare its teeth, gnashing *(Be still, child)* this knot of constellations: absurd, enchanting. The tangled placebo (our guttural sounds) of me and you and everyone we know. A room of voices. A dark room, a blind man, a black cat that is both there and not there. Round and round; don't worry, by now I know the drill — *when you cross the threshold, close your eyes.* As in: listen for that sound, the sound of stars raveling. As in, the knots in trees scraping bits of stardust from the ether. As in: show your teeth. Smile.

Cassidy Parong

---

1 *Further* was the name of Ken Kesey's bus
2 Russell Edson, "The Reason Why the Closet-Man Is Never Sad"
3 love, agony; call it what you will

Accidental Death

How she would've laughed—
        told the story to her dog
                as they walked

by the pond skimmed
        by a net of dragonflies
                stitching an insect quilt—

if she was alive
        and heard how autocorrect
                converted *Mary Oliver*

to *bury all of her,*
        the dog snapping at fliers
                too adept to be caught

until—flying backwards—
        one was, then she'd brace
                open the jaws to extract it.

David Sullivan

−photo, Nina Koocher, Provincetown MA

Freeway Dog

Even with the virus there is still enough freeway
traffic to smush my thoughts, my ideas, my fantasies
of writing a good poem.

The origin of imagination
fades with the thrum of speeding
tires. A dog darts across
three lanes . . . and makes it.
Luck has nothing to do with it.
I smile.

Linda Serrato

Betwixt

Privileged States of Being During a 21st-Century Pandemic in the US of A

LIMBO —shimmy under the 12-foot-long stick at least 3 feet off of ground zero, which could be the floor or a flattened curve in a pandemic if you are thinking of going to heaven.

IN-BETWEEN TIMES — the euroasian middle ages, also known as medieval times or the dark ages due to plague, reign of christianity and the catholic church.

INTERSTITIAL — finding the space separating things, discerning the physics of the vacuum, spacing out. Is it a particle or a wave?

THRESHOLD — on the edge of something, leaving something, leading to somewhere else.

LIMINAL — dreamwork, meditation, chanting, mandala gazing, get into those beta waves because the beaches are closed.

NAP — don't go to sleep if you're too tired, download some deep breathing exercises instead of closing your eyes.

LACUNAE — write a poem about the insects, their work in the soil, in the garden; the invisible ones like the nurses' aides, the radiology techs, bus drivers, grocery clerks, janitors, cleaners who are mostly black and brown people.

TIME OUT — stop the game, play a musical instrument; if you are not musical, try a kazoo or a drum; pots and pans work well for timpani.

LAYOFF — you get unemployment plus $600 but it might not happen until 2023. if you do get it, it will end too soon.

INTERMEZZO – look up words when you don't know the exact (or inexact) definition, like *discomfit*.

RECESS – go outside and get some fresh air even if you just stick your head out the window or your toes out the door; stand in your bare feet on dirt, or better yet, sand.

LET UP – no pain, no pain; don't do any exercises that hurt because you can't afford purgatory or to try to get help in an emergency room.

SPELLS – magic lexicon, think of new ways to spell things, like *won* and *wonder*, *wand* and *wander*.

DOLDRUMS – even though it refers to a quieted sea, think of it as cave training.

INTERMISSION – if you decide to take up the quest, this page will immolate in 30 seconds.

SUSPENSION – bridges the in-between and either end of the interstitial.

BREATHER – humming from the back of your throat while burning sage and rosemary, a bronchial dilator which might help after your non-nap meditation.

COMMA – a brief reprise, coasting from one phrase to another.

PERIOD – the next capital letter will begin soon.

STOP SIGN – just a momentary reprieve, a memory lapse, of our dependence on fossil fuels.

HALFTIME – so you can get more snacks or pee before play resumes.

DIET – too many snacks: too much stress, too little discipline.

CREVASS CREVICE CHASM — opening the burden of mystery, might be a Keats phrase.

HOLDING PATTERN — circling overhead, could be birds, planes or the stars; just consider it.

STOPOVER — a break, sensory deprivation or delay, preventing return to normalcy.

WAITING ROOM — before you see the doctor, get the news, hold in the Zoom Room.

AT THE GATE — getting ready.

ON YOUR MARKS — toe the line.

WAIT A MINUTE — new information arrives.

LOUNGE — an actual place meant for non-medieval in-between times.

A GOOD CRY — how long can this go on? how long has this been going on?

LENT — a fast between dramatic events.

SLOWDOWN — less work, you may have some time.

ECHO — craving a long drag on a cigarette. Smoke, not flame.

INTERIM — inner looking, a black hole, a doughnut.

REST — not a nap, action between notes on little pieces of paper that become this.

Kat Brown

–sculpture, Nora Sarkissian

15

It's hard to write about dragons—they are extravagant,
unruly and come in so many colors. My favorite is the
Tibetan turquoise dragon: it protects against discord of
all kinds. It also protects against "especially slanderous
gossip and the misuse of words."

The turquoise dragon has a legendary love of music;
(mine is partial to Arvo Pärt, especially "Für Alina").
It flies (not all dragons do), most beautifully flies.
I saw it just now, outside my window, pivoting around
a star, around all of creation, its sulfurous breath spewing
hellfire and lightning.

O great serpent, my friend, set my life on fire.

Lauren Crux
excerpt from "Little Rambles"

My Cat

My cat he has four corners
and a leg depends from each.
His head is like a grapefruit
but fuzzy as a peach.

And at the end of every leg
a double paw has he —
More claws, and all the better
for climbing up my knee.

His whiskers clean and wiry,
ears soft and free of mite.
His tail has a decided kink,
it's banded, black on white.

My cat his name is Ogden,
a loaf of fur and fat.
Sometimes he'll chase a cricket,
but God forbid a rat.

My cat he has four corners,
four corners has my cat.
He has a kitty box indoors
but prefers the yard for that.

Ron Arruda

Pets are a great comfort in times of stress. -RA

Bobble Buddha–photo, Kate Aver Avraham

6

Finally! Rain at 6:50 a.m., Feb. 2, 2014.
Groundhog Day, Santa Cruz. I'm up early,
reading, writing. The boy cat is frapping.

A cat needs to frap (Frenetic Random Activity Periods)
to keep its neurocircuitry working. It is not having fun.
Those of us watching are usually laughing, however.

Frapping is not play: play involves galumphing,
which is fun. This distinction seems important—like
the difference between a bread knife and a tomato
knife. Each has a distinct function even if they look
somewhat alike.

Would that I could, when faced with the unbearable,
fling myself into the air, gyrate and yowl. Streak
about in a crazed frenzy. Then be done with it.
Then take a nap.

A cat has to frap (and nap) to be a cat.
A human has to be kind to be human.

Lauren Crux
excerpt from "Little Rambles"

Certificate of Playfulness

The Bearer of this Document
is a Lifetime Member in Good Standing of
THE SOCIETY OF PLAYFUL SPIRITS
and even in a Pandemic
is hereby and forever entitled to . . .

Walk in the rain; jump in mud puddles; blow bubbles;
Stop along the way; go barefoot; watch the stars come out;
Go on adventures; say hello to everyone;
Take bubble baths; sing in the shower;
Have a merry heart in spite of it all;
Read children's books; act silly; wander around;
Wear wild socks; dance on a whim; fly kites;
Laugh & cry for the health of it;
Give up worry and guilt and shame;
Say *yes*; say *no*; say the magic word;
Ask lots of questions; see things differently;
Climb a tree; ride a bicycle;
Fall down and get up again;
Talk with animals; talk to the universe; listen to the wind;
Do nothing; daydream; play with toys;
Stay up late; take naps;
Get excited about everything; listen to music;
Enjoy having a body;
Make up new rules; tell stories . . .

. . . And do anything else that may safely bring you and others
More happiness, celebration, joy, health,
love, creativity and grace!

Mary Kay Hamilton
Mutual Fun Manager

Trust–Sarah Bianco

IT SINGS
of the
EARTH

Earth Abides

strong silent soft long
before we came it will be
here after we're gone

Bob Nielsen

Sometimes you just have to dive down into it

into the murky waters of the news swirl that surrounds your ears and
you let your whole body be inside the brown black unseeable water
of all the things we have done and all the scary fears that ever crossed
your mind

diving into the wreck

yet the body has the will and the way to swim up for air just in time to
see that sky can still be blue you can breathe your breath that inhale
and exhale there you go onto land now warm sand and the nestle of
the rustle of trees birds sing

open your eyes to this

Jean Mahoney

Landscape
after a poem by Julie Cadwallader Staub

Drawn to water–
not immense undulating seas
where horizons fade, but the
dank bio-webs, marsh and
wetland where currents
quiver, heron and hawk,
egret and owl ply the shallows
and banks, where grackles nest
the reeds, swallows in the
eves,
and otter and beaver,
bass and bluegill live as
they live.

This is the landscape
that carries me beyond
the light
of my understanding
into the willowy shadows, shapes
shifting, the unknown lay of the
river where one draws back,
hesitates,
or plunges deep the oars,
pulling hard and steady, feels
the resistance,
sees the *bend*
in the river . . . and
still says yes.

Gail Brenner

Big River–photo, Lauren Crux

be gentle, ziggurat

cusp inversion, like moving in water: the small gods of your fingers
drum scriptures into calloused skin

you don't flinch (it doesn't hurt) but shudder knowing the world
wakes in symbols, 1,000 bird-creatures caw at the cuticle

emerging from swollen pearls. you let them, because you are lonely
and your throat too sore to sing

if only they could carve softness: clouds or sand dunes, the curve
of a leaf floating atop still waters

if only they knew kindness: the warm drip of honey, or the voice
of your mother: a memory of river in the middle of the sea

Cassidy Parong

Iris

So what if I don't want to be
connected to the rest of the globe?

And what if I do think the iris
the most beautiful thing
and not the speed of data
flapping its wings?

So what if I go home
to the silence snow taught me
and the warm cat sleeping
when the crowd's going out.

I circle in search of a place
to be still
to feel the earth turn
and count the slow clouds
as they pass.

Maggie Paul
from Borrowed World
Hummingbird Press

She Stands–photo, Melody Culver

Tree of Life

I dreamt I was a tree
and in my mind's eye
watched my toiling roots –
(dark coils clinging to earth,
anchoring existence)
my gnarled and knobby fingers
searching for nourishment

I saw my trunk
with craggy bark pecked
and pebbled by a thousand birds –
(a haven for every insect
crawling and flying)
but sturdy still

And reaching up and out
my tangle of cool limbs
fed by amber sap
that flowed from root
to tip (sweet dark wine
of the underground)

At the end of each branch –
audacious green leaves
(at once both smooth and veined)
making love with the sun

And my final crown of dazzling blooms
(glorious in their vanity)
enticing hummingbird and honey bee
who, in carrying off each tiny seed
become partners for life
in yet another tree

Waking then, I knew . . .
hold on, stand tall
reach out, love deep
feed and be fed
bloom

Be a tree

Deborah Wenzler

Memory Bank

I will spend this morning in the shadow of Morro Rock.

The sun treads a jeweled path across the bay
illuminating slow-moving trawlers
returning at dawn.

An arrow of pelicans lifts in silent unison,
momentarily darkening the sky,

as three otters, wearing sea-shined pelts, slip
in and out of quiet waters.

A solitary fisherman casts and recasts from the jetty,
catching his breath, but nothing more.

We spend our lifetimes collecting memories.

Quiet moments become our currency –
easily withdrawn when needed
to pay down grief and loneliness.

Memories are a well –
cool and deep,
from which we drink
when pain parches our lips
and burns our skin.

Memories are light –
chasing down sadness
when it follows us, close as shadows
that lengthen and distort
as evening arrives.

Deborah Wenzler

The Murmurings of Roots

Will your cravings ever leave you,
lifting like a startled flock
from your naked limbs?
Will your mind finally come to rest
one ordinary morning
in your mantra?
What might you hear in the sheer silence?

Your heartbeat –
and the squirrel's,
the secret language of the garden,
what the earthworms say to the roots.
You were waiting for the voice of God,
and here in the cave of your heart
is the alleluia of the blackberry
at the moment it plumps into perfect ripeness
and the Deo gratias of the squirrel
as it plucks the berry from the vine.

Attune your breath to the cedar's sigh
and rise from your cushion now
before the diamond dewdrops
on the sour grass dry.

Mary Camille Thomas

Indra's Web
In nature, nothing exists alone –Rachel Carson

I'm a 6,000 year old woman looking for sanctuary
in an age that no longer cares about earth's story.
The past's childhood is lost, a memory we press
down like rumpled fall leaves in a scrap pile.
I lean into the wind which forces me to button
looking for my tree self, my tree self,
our relationship tentative with longing.

The way in is the way out as any tree knows
tunneling down to the deepest roots
then extending out of its single treeness
to the other roots, all their wild selves
entangled, comforting each shoot
every seed and leaf and petal
the crown of Indra's web.

In the mind of the many
there exists a great divide
a split in the reptilian brain
that has never healed
an intrinsic loneliness
a virus has reappeared
as it has through evolution
bringing a great pause
a gap in our storyline
time to listen to trees
the soul's heartbeat

The filaments of trees
tunnel through time and space
up to stars which exploded
millions of years ago,
dispersing iron and stardust
inside the trees, inside
the human heart
all beings connected
hope is not an end state
but an entrance to grace.

I am a 6,000 year old woman
carrying nature's seeds of hope
and this is her tale.
We are out of desire
for extinction.
The impulse for life
is a poem in the blood,
the spirit avoiding capture.

Sandia Belgrade
July 26,2020

Richardson Grove

Oh, these trees,
red and brown, weathered and grey
line the road like devoted greeters
standing at the entrance of long-aisled church.

From within their sole majesty,
the breath of god rises into the deep and steadfast sky.

Seldom knowing death, only tarnished by fire,
the cathedrals, candelabras, and clans grow side by side,
sharing the well of fog that nourishes their thick and ancient bodies.

Their seemingly endless trunks and full branches
stretch like a clade of dinosaurs whose faces we no longer see.

Tall fern and grass, refuge for caterpillar and mice,
know their place here, as do deer and rabbit.

A red-tailed hawk in slow flight bows to the feast of ground below.

This sanctuary, resonant with life and holy in its silence,
soothes and quiets the expectant traveler.

The door to heaven opens.
A small heart grows wide.

Karen Bartholomew

Trees, UCSD–photo, Lauren Crux

Tiny Miracles

...what we get is just what we're willing to find:
small wonders, where they grow. –Barbara Kingsolver

Today I worship at the altar of lilies.
Rust-hued bearded irises defy gravity,
levitate gold striated blooms
above pink and yellow snapdragons,
molting remains of blue floss flower.

Garden goliaths throw shade
upon white alyssum, hyacinths,
daffodils, dwarf freckled foxglove.

Lavender wisteria unfolds
miniature Japanese lanterns.
Six weeks of sheltering in place
alters daily routine, improves meditation.

I rejoice at red and purple salvia,
the minuscule hummingbirds they attract,
give thanks for tiny miracles,
fragrant herbs, color-splashed garden.

Jennifer Lagier

Mendocino–photo, Lauren Crux

I Wanted Many Things

That is the human way.
Some were for me, many for others
None were material, all were for ease, peace,
Openheartedness, ability, fortitude, success.

I made stories and saw myself
And my dear ones in them.
This too is the human way.
It is a delight, until it is a straitjacket.
All things that deviate from the story
Are rejected, called ugly, feared.

I wonder how to bend
As the birch tree bends with the wind,
Relinquish ideas and stories,
And bend into the living Earth.
I bow to my stories,
Then gently put them away.

There is a candle lit before me,
the dancing movement of Now.
In the garden there is more life than I can hold.
It sings of the Earth,
The only story that holds.

Carolyn Brigit Flynn

Ode to the Marigold

Flower of the Earth, found in every country.
    There is history of healing in the marigold
        through its herbal qualities.

Coming from elongated black and beige pips,
    marigolds orange and ginger with feathery leaves
        share their bloom with me in spring, summer, autumn.

Seeds gathered by my hand from a neighbor's garden,
    stored in an envelope over the winter –
        anticipate bringing me joy in their growth.

The process:
    watch,
    wait as seedlings reach from the soil in green plumage,
        explode like fireworks shot from carroty tufts,
        burst into a blast of yellow and rust.

Marigolds set a boundary with their scent.
    They confront me as sun-gold petals tickle my nostrils,
        while shooing away unwelcome pests.

In the end new seeds close in on themselves,
        cycle into fawn-colored pods that create contrast,
        soften the gilded auburn vivacity of growth,
        move back to their source.

Joan Donato
Gifts from the pandemic to nurture my creative child -JD

Bedside Flowers–painting, Sonia Calderón

Seed Money

At noon I shut off
the politicians.
I'll probably never understand—
their solutions
hammered from plywood
like broken windows covered over.

I remember the sunflower head,
large as a dinner plate,
drying on the stump,
honeycomb patches
already being picked clean
by blue jays and blackbirds

Outside, gray-striped seeds
ping into my jelly jar
like seed money
as more of the intricate
sunflower pattern emerges
where hundreds of seeds fit together.
Enough to share with the birds.

I pluck out a supply
of what remains
for a future with a windfall
of sunflowers, one thing
I can count on.

Bernice Rendrick

Dear Mary Oliver

You would be proud of me.
    Today I stopped what I was doing to go outside
    knowing the trumpet vines were singing over the fence
    in summer sunlight
    and I would be a fool not to go out there
    and clap for them.

Other surprises revealed themselves
    as if I had just stepped into an open meadow
    after having been lost for a long time
    in a dark forest.

The burnished afternoon light
    drenching the mountaintops in gold.
A soft breeze
    creating music of its own
    through the eucalyptus foliage.
A birdsong I had never heard before
    making landfall on my heart.
Tiny insects with iridescent wings
    coming to visit my paper.
Pink forget-me-nots growing out of nearby rocks.

Have I gone mad not to have noticed all along
    this abundance of riches
    this bountiful harvest
    this preponderance of joy
    the way each morning lands on our doorstep
    waiting for us to cry out
Hallelujah for all this beauty?

Sarojani Rohan

Hope Blooms–photo, Jan Rupp

During the shelter in place, we all had to simplify our lives, adjust to social distancing, and yet keep connected to our world. Walking amidst the wonders of nature and photographing the beauty around us, unchanged by the virus, sparked enjoyment and great hope for better days. -JR

–photo, Nina Koocher, Santa Cruz CA

the hummingbirds keep visiting me on my third floor apartment

they're searching for the sweetness in my home
    already they've sucked dry a blossomed orange tree
        —no energy left in its roots to become sour or bitter—
            just dry and coarse. its pores cracking together into
                veins, canyons in a corpse for the ants to inhabit

one rests on an empty pot, catching her breath and looking
    at me the man across the street is watering the cement
        too hopeful for the cracks in sidewalks to bloom
            with rogue dandelions
            —o bird can't you see his flaming nasturtium?
                they are where the sun sleeps!
                    she casts a gaze at the blushing plants
                    and back to me, unconvinced

it's seven o'clock now and my feet are still sockless
    and i'm smoking until i can feel my lungs again
    the humming bird floats forward,
        sprinting through this cloud of breath
        within kissing distance she stays and stares at me
            inspecting the vacuumed parts of my self

Clem Peterson

Hope Springs

Spring has come early this year –
tender buds are breaking on every bough
and the tears of winter are long dry –

Look! all the yellow-faced flowers
are throwing their dust skyward –
wood sorrel and wild mustard,
scotch broom and mock orange

Lusty seeds of hope rising like small-petaled suns

the earth is singing green
in emerald notes that carpet
hill and field and weedy roadside –

all this against a trembling sky –
a pale blue sigh striped
with brush strokes of white cloud –

and in its crescent-shaped cage
my heart aches
from the beauty of it all.

Deborah Wenzler

summer twenty twenty

Beyond our door
bloom salvia flowers,
all musk and sweetness,
dancing on the spike
of a hummingbird's tongue.

Up the throat
comes a rusty-hinged sound.
Take my hand past the sadness.
Even now, I still believe
that everything wants to be singing.

Kim Ly Bui

Already There

The wild geese are heading home over Truro dunes,
those rolling breasts of sand that have nourished my soul.
When did I first suckle there?
In college perhaps, with Martha.
When we slept out under the dark star-strewn sky
letting the earth hold us in her embrace.
Gypsies of our own making
in a world we were reinventing.

Suddenly rudely awakened by the local authority
kicking at our heels: No sleeping here.
And we left, delighted in our delinquency.

Little did I understand the delicacy of the dunes.
That they might drift away, carried off by the wind.
Back then we were free
to roam and race and fall amongst their undulations.
Our innocence was true.

Then came preservation.
The need to replant the grasses
to hold the land in place. Slowly
the land emerges as it used to be
and will become again.

Now, a path wanders through the gritty moonscape,
a miraculous journey that leads one out to the sea.
To the edge of the continent where the dune shacks sit
straining for a whiff of Portugal.

If you walk along the water's edge
you might make it down to the sand bars that appear at low tide.
And if you are lucky,
on a given day, they may be covered with seals basking in the sun,
falling into the water as sand gives way beneath them.

Sometimes these same seals
show up bay side, at high tide, uncomfortably close to shore.
A warning to unsuspecting children
that the sharks may not be far behind.

Bay side where, when Josh was young,
he and I were surrounded by iridescent baby squid
caught amongst the tide pools,
shimmering in the sun like opalescent jewels.

We squealed with delight to witness such a sight
and to celebrate the union of mother and child.

Years later as Bernie and I walked the beaches further south
we found flounder stranded amongst these pools,
and the next day schools of dog sharks,
and two months later on a winter's day the jawbones of those sharks.

The sharks who had followed the flounder in were stranded there
themselves. Left to dry out on the belly of the land.

And always the terns and sandpipers and hermit crabs that travel
in and out with the tide, telling time by the sun
and moon and whispering wind.
The wild geese may be heading home but I am already there.

Nina Koocher

–photo, Nina Koocher, Truro MA

Love Poem

Usually it's morning when he studies his reflection with the seriousness of an autumn-aged man staring down mortality. It's morning and winter's sun has just given off a glint of passion, covering the silent hill sheltered in half-light. He is my first visitor, my morning guest, the point Eros aims her arrow at. And I am in love with him.

This afternoon, I am twice lucky! While the shivering sun sinks, the great blue heron appears again. There are two of him when he bows down, two of him in prayer, preying on the crayfish and other small swimmers in the pond. I see him twice, embrace him twice, imagine him in a family instead of alone, like me. I imagine him surrounded by herons following his cue, waiting to feed while he feeds first. For a moment he steps behind the five-foot tules and disappears, but my love calls him back. It must be love, because the sight of him makes a miracle in me. And isn't that what love is: surprise and wonder at the very thing that stays.

Maggie Paul
from Scrimshaw
Hummingbird Press

Great Blue Heron–photo, Gail Brenner
Sandmound Slough, Sacramento Delta

Encounter

After another difficult day, I head out to empty the compost at dusk. I've decided I have what a friend has coined OTSD: Ongoing Traumatic Stress Disorder. Our earth is being pummeled. A couple of years ago this toxicity snuck into my gut as an overgrowth of bacteria, causing intense cyclical pain. And subsequent solitude. My gait has slowed.

I follow the backyard deck that borders Rodeo Gulch, a grassy riparian corridor. Just as I'm about to step off into the wet weeds, I look up. A huge red-tailed hawk stands on a small mound of dirt ten feet away. It flutters its wings as I say softly, "Oh, hello beautiful," folding my body to sit at ground level. We are now eye to eye. Motionless.

I talk to animals and mountains. Why just look when you can have a conversation? I breathe, become very quiet, pre-verbal. The hawk watches with its intense chestnut-brown gaze.

Silently I say, "You are magnificent, thank you, thank you."

Gratitude floods out of me. Here we are, face to face, with no hint of aggression. I drop my caution further and move into love.

"Are you okay?" I ask. "Am I?"

And now I am weeping. Crying for myself but especially for the hawk, as its shrinking local habitat mirrors the planet plummeting into unparalleled degradation. "I am so sorry, so sorry."

The hawk tilts its head slightly and I hear, "strength…perseverance." I am desperate for the hawk to know my complicity, and in the same ragged breath, my devotion.

But the hawk is not concerned. It just is and this is-ness wipes the tears right out of me. We sit in the spacious moment. In this silence I hear from the hawk, "wider view." A true citizen of the skies. The hawk says "beauty," says "gift." We crouch together for thirty wondrous minutes.

The raptor spreads its large wings and hops onto a potted barrel cactus, planted decades ago. My partner joins us. "So regal!" He talks aloud for another twenty minutes to the hawk.

We wonder if this bird is sick or injured, but don't think so. A few years ago we thought the same thing about a hawk, not moving, with wings splayed, in our Monterey pine tree. We dragged a huge ladder up to the tree to save it, only to find another hawk there, wings fully open. I had climbed into a sex scene. And then there was the time a Cooper's hawk crashed into our window then, disoriented, fumbled into the garage. We did manage to corner that raptor, bringing it to Native Animal Rescue for overnight observation and release. That hawk came back and spent the summer hanging close with us. We were all smitten.

As the first star shimmers above us, the red-tailed hawk lifts up and floats to the meadow. Two days later a large raptor circles in big sweeping arcs, ignoring two dive-bombing crows. It has sailed from the eucalyptus stand across the watershed. A giant nest is lodged in a crook of branches, swaying in the early spring wind.

Later that week, in pain, in the middle of the night, the hawk lands in my mind. "Strength," it says. It says, "perseverance, gift, beauty." I slow my breath, look for the wider view.

Dyana Basist

Night blooms the Iris

In the quiet dark and predawn hours,
while the insects float the
air with clicking beats of rubbed wings,
I walk out to see the stars and
notice the root beer-scented iris has
unfolded its flower and
furry petals,

shed its papery wrap
into the secret beauty
of its green fuse
through the misty veil of night.

Do we unfold our secret beauty in
the cool stillness of night,
cooked in dreams and rhythmic breathing,
baked in the alchemy of dark
through this pandemic
when the streets abandon themselves to wild creatures?

Does the quiet call the blossom into its revealing,
or the soft rattle of instincts,
or is it the stars and planets aligned
in the deep of the dark round of new moon?

Opening to the mystery
I find myself in alertness,
listening, reflecting,

while the dark is moved by the singing of birds.

Susan Heinz
4/23/20

−photo, Nina Koocher, Santa Cruz CA

Ordinary

Six inches of dull brown
from her beak to long dark tail,
she comes every day
to the mat by my glass door
after bully scrub jays
have left only husks of seeds.

Not a purple finch, yellow oriole,
or red-capped woodpecker,
but amusing with spindly feet
and rusty streaked throat
that marks her breast.

She is cautious, sneaks up
to snack with no others nearby.
When I leave the door open,
she sometimes wanders inside,
explores, then retreats,
occasionally brings her fledglings
with their beige under-fluff to dine.

Year-round visitor to my porch
she reminds me how I always thought
I was like her, not colorful,
a humdrum sort in high school.
She persuades me now
that being ordinary is exceptional.

Laura Bayless

i keep counting my blessings

watching the clouds change
    tasting the fresh sun
      after days of rain
          it grows and grows and grows

every day i see murmurations of red winged blackbirds
  and i listen to the humming ones catch their breath

    so many birds
      and sights of flight

    i want to taste their freedom
     let the wind inhabit me
        —like shelley and keats dreamed of

wondering and worrying for the day
  i cannot see what flowers grow
  beneath my treading feet

Clem Peterson

Turtle Island

What if the world
      was created by a giant turtle
          swimming across the sky
              at the beginning of time?

What if the turtle
      carried dreams in her belly,
          giving birth to fish and stars?

What if the high flying tern
      marked the world lines of space and time
          with nets of aurora borealis?

What if the donkey said
      the humans are a joke, spinning through space
          juggling fire and ice?

What if the crab said
      crawl sideways if you want to uncover
          the dreams that are painted inside of shells?

What if the moon said
      the night will tell you secrets
          if you listen to the music inside of stones?

What if the shark said
      you will discover fish that glow like lanterns
          in deeper currents of ocean water?

What if the octopus said
    your dreams are tentacles
        into a future filled with fish and golden apples?

What if the turtle
    keeps swimming out of the sky
        to a universe hidden somewhere else?

What if the buffalos
    stampede with their ancestors across the Great Plains
        under an ocean of sky?

Buffalo Woman says
    the world is a dream or nightmare.
        Weave your visions with tender hands.

Diane Frank

Spirit Dancer

What a grasshopper sees
in the light,
on the dew,
in the morning,
is blue.

a circle, a sphere
a dream begins here,
where nothing exists but what the heart feels
like the pulse of tall grass
succumbs to the fields.

What the day brings
with its yellow and gray shield,
we might know if we watch a grasshopper dance
through tiny clear hoops-
first slow... and then fast.

A vision of sorts,
moving past what is visible
into what is unseen,
except by the ones who hear the sound,
the hum of the world in its wake.

The splash of water to air,
the little "thump"
a drop makes
when it lands on a leaf
and awaits the touch of green
from above and green from beneath.

Small head, small legs,
Small body with wings,
you are a reason
the great earth sings!

Karen Bartholomew

Newly Born Comes to the River–photo, Deena Metzger

19

Last night a new friend, painter from Germany,
said she found that our northern California landscape
stripped her of all that was familiar—a big city, a
bicycle, constant movement, phone calls, emails . . .

Here in acres of undeveloped land, filled with coyotes
and bobcats and mountain lions and deer and red-tailed
hawks and white-tailed rabbits and purple finches and
blue jays and rattlesnakes and endless pill bugs and a
dog named Hank and a kind man named Tom, she lost
her familiar ways of escape. In all this silence, she fell
back on herself. Discovering what she was made of
without all the props. "And this is a good thing," she
declared. "But I still don't like the snakes."

I'm okay with the snakes. As a kindness to my friend,
I walk in front so they will strike me first.

Lauren Crux
Excerpt from "Little Rambles"

Borrow the Earth–Mixed Media series, Nancy Jones
For the 100th Anniversary of Women's Right to Vote
Photo credit: George A Smathers Library, University of Florida

It seems to me that the earth may be borrowed but not bought. It may be used but not owned. It gives itself in response to love and tending, offers its seasonal flowering and fruiting. But we are tenants and not possessors, lovers and not masters.

—Marjorie Kinnan Rawlings, author, 1896-1953

A Shared Boat

I have a fierce love for this earth
  Which means I cannot be a bystander
    Which means I must not be silent or separate
      What we love we will not turn away from

We are in the midst of a phenomenon related to PTSD (Post Traumatic Stress Disorder), but instead of it being post, it has become an ongoing traumatic stress. Climate disruption, mass extinctions, and now a pandemic. Witnessing destruction and feeling the earth's pain has become an affliction. I am giving it a name: OTSD, Ongoing Transitional Stress Disorder. Change is coming, ready or not. If we resist, like pain, it only worsens.

How can we, how can I, sustain myself without turning away? I ground myself in creative acts, in the dream state, in the language of flesh.

And I turn to the natural world for which I grieve, as it has always been my teacher.

Like a doe at the meadow's edge, I listen for whether to step boldly into the clearing or melt back into shadow. I absorb a mother bear's fierce protectiveness. I take on a plant-like sensibility, softening like cottonwood leaves in a puddle. I sniff the air like a wolf, to alert my pack of safety and danger. As darkness descends, we howl, our voices covering distance until we know we are not alone.

In the biblical story, Noah's Ark only held a chosen few. As habitats decline and the seas rise around us, we need a shared boat that holds us all, that looks more like a cradle than a battleship. Separate, we are lost. If we travel light, holding each other, the rising tide can lift us from the muddy banks into the current. The river, never lost, always finds its way.

  What we love we will not turn away from
    Which means we must not be silent or separate
  We cannot be alone in these times
As we fiercely love our world

Marilyn DuHamel

Parts of this essay are from the vision statement for my blog, Earth Dialogues, which emerged out of my anguish at hearing the UN Climate Report warning that we have twelve years *to act on behalf of this beautiful earth we humans share with all other beings. -MDH*

Who We Will Become:
Reflections on Human Destiny

Bring to mind – Herds of caribou, crossing a matted and soggy tundra, outnumbering the scope of your sight, their breath rising, a warm and visible fog of life hovering over the frozen ground; their clattering antlers and sturdy hoofbeats thundering low in your ears.

Bring to mind – Great whales crossing unmeasured terrains of ocean, their sonar songs reaching out to each other across miles of empty dark sea, bearing both water and the need for air as they rise and fall and push on under sun or stars, never doubting their journey to a Home both known and unknown.

Bring to mind – Birds; flying birds, the sky thick with wings and tireless flapping. Follow them high as they hollow the space they fill, neither food nor water to end their fainting, and still they go, undaunted and bold, bearing their intercontinental assignments.

Then in that great company, commit yourself here, on this Earth, at this time, a willing pilgrim in a Great Human Migration to a new way of life, walking a ground littered with all we are shedding and yet to be shed.

We've our fierce hearts to guide us, inestimable Love to fuel us, and the seeds planted long ago in our Souls to grow us into who we will become.

Donna Runnalls

Yosemite Falls–photo, Kate Aver Avraham

About the
ARTISTS
& AUTHORS

Lalo Alvarez came to the United States illegally as a child. At the age of 14 he dropped out of high school to work and contribute to the family. His mother, Lucia, who was the best person in the world, had only a fourth-grade education but she taught Lalo how to dance, to be happy and to love. Lalo will follow in her footsteps until he dies.

Beth Appleton I was born in California but now live as an artist along Florida's Gulf Coast. Here, I delight in tiny marine life and stand in awe of infinite sky. My life is full of stories that weave through my work. Art is intuitive, exhilarating and good for the soul. bethappleton.net

Ron Arruda moved to Santa Cruz some 30 years ago from Massachusetts, to go back to school and to make a new life. It worked! After 15 years as a curator at the UCSC Arboretum, he retired in 2009 and continues a deeply miscellaneous life, centered on daily bike rides to the beach. The best things in life are free!

Kate Aver Avraham began her love relationship with words as a toddler, rewriting all her picture books! She has three published children's books, including *What Will You Be, Sara Mee?* (Charlesbridge). Her poems have found homes in numerous journals and anthologies. Blue Light Press will publish her poetry book, *Arms of My Longing*, in 2021. Kate is a native of Santa Cruz now living in Aptos amidst the redwoods.

Born and raised in Switzerland, **Ursi Barshi-Vogel** spent 35 years in the US before returning to her hometown, where she enjoys walking and taking public transportation past historic buildings, the beauty of the mountains within reach. She is fortunate to have been in a writing group with Carolyn Brigit Flynn, which nurtured her love for words. She is a published poet who strives to express her personal feelings and thoughts in a way that lifts them into a collective sensitivity.

Karen Bartholomew lives in rural Michigan, where she writes fiction, poetry and songs. She is inspired by the perfection and beauty of the natural world as it reflects human existence. She is known in her local community as the human mother to a love-dog named Lucy the Mighty Chihuahua.

Dyana Basist lives in Santa Cruz CA on Rodeo Gulch, a riparian corridor. Her garden and bordering wild lands provide a continual source of support and inspiration. Dyana's new book, *Coyote Wind*, celebrates her rollicking long-term love affair with Coyote, both the mythic and the not-so mythic. It is available through the author at openmesa@sbcglobal.net. To learn more about haiku, the Yuki Teikei Haiku Society's website is youngleaves.org

Ellen Bass A Chancellor of the Academy of American Poets, Ellen' most recent book is *Indigo* (Copper Canyon, 2020). Her poems regularly appear in *The New Yorker* and *American Poetry Review*. She coedited the first major anthology of women's poetry, *No More Masks!* and cowrote the groundbreaking *The Courage to Heal*. She teaches in Pacific University's MFA program.

Enid Baxter Ryce has exhibited at museums internationally and has been written about in *The New York Times, Los Angeles Times, Artforum* and others. She has won awards for her work as an artist and educator. She lives in Marina, CA with her family and is a professor at CSUMB.

Laura Bayless is the author of four collections of poetry, *The Edge of the Nest, White Streams and Touchstones, Persistent Dreams*, and *Chairs in the River*. Her poems have appeared in many local and national publications including *Porter Gulch Review, Blue Heron*, and the *Homestead Review*. She has found the making of a poem to be a mysterious process, a delicate balance of the strange and the familiar.

Sandia Belgrade I live at 8,000 feet in the Rockies with 85 degrees one day and 20 degrees and snow the next. During a quarantine. This means I am species adaptable. Able to write both poetry and fiction: two novels, several poetry books and a translation, some published, all contributing to a very interesting life.

Sarah Bianco is a painter, residing at the Tannery Arts Center, in Santa Cruz, CA. She works out of her studio there, called Apricity Gallery. Her painting ranges from smaller works on canvas or panel to large-scale murals and house painting with her business, Painting by Bianco. She loves to participate in community events and collaborations, spend time in nature, and hang out with her puppy.

Gail Brenner is a writer and educator from Santa Cruz, CA. Her poetry has appeared in *Porter Gulch Review* and *phren-Z*; the anthology *Sisters Singing*; and on the National Writers Union website. She is the author of *English for Dummies*; *Webster's New World American Idioms Handbook*; and *Master the TOEFL*. Gail teaches in the Writing Program and the Dept. of Languages and Applied Linguistics at UCSC. She finds enduring hope, resilience and renewal in the stalwart redwoods, fragile beauty of wetlands, and magnificent biodiversity on the edge of the continent.

Kat Brown is an avid gardener, writer and poet living on Awaswas territory in the foothills of the Santa Cruz mountains.

Peggy Bryan, born on a summer day in Santa Cruz, three days later moved into a knotty pine cabin in the Sierras where her dad worked at a sawmill. Living half the year near the beach and half in the heart of the forest influences her to this day. She's an ordained Episcopal priest leading a jail/reentry ministry.

Sonia Calderón was born in Berkeley, CA and raised in Minneapolis, MN, where she started exploring her artistic side at a young age. Calderón's interests include fashion, design, mysteries of nature, and the human experience. Her artistic influences are several abstract expressionistic painters of the 20th century, street photographers who focus on glam and guilty pleasures. soniacalderon.design

Norine Cardea is a mother, grandmother, mental health therapist, Family Constellation facilitator, community elder, and artist.

Johanna Courtleigh is a Licensed Professional Counselor, hypnotherapist, writer and solo performance artist in Portland, OR. Her works seeks to help people heal from the mistruths they were taught, and come to a core of deeper reverence, self-love, awareness, ease and integrity—internally, and in their relationships with others. jcourtleigh.com

Lauren Crux at any given moment, is a writer, performer, storyteller, photographer, psychotherapist, adventurer, and someone committed to Good and Necessary Trouble. Her poetry, prose, and photography have been published in numerous journals and anthologies. She lives in Santa Cruz, CA where alas, during the pandemic, she is busy aging in place.

Melody Culver is a longtime writer with Carolyn Flynn's writing group. She is an adoring grandmother, a copy editor obsessed with her new dictionary, and an author liaison for self-publishing. She feels lucky and grateful to collude with Kate Avraham on this anthology. Shout out to her Indiana family!

d'vorah darvie, bronx native; santa cruz has her heart, longtime home to family of friends. color and beauty of the natural world is her muse, weaving the textures and patterns of inspiration in whatever medium she uses.

Dinah Davis moved to the Central Coast 10 years ago after retiring from a career in education. She has two sons and five grandchildren whom she misses seeing during COVID. She started writing 6 years ago upon discovering boxes filled with old letters, clippings and notebooks from her parents dating back to the 1920s. She since completed a memoir dedicated to both their lives, *River of Faith*. Dinah lives in Aptos CA with her partner, Sally, and Yorkie, Trix.

Laura Davis, author of seven bestselling nonfiction books, including *The Courage to Heal* and *I Thought We'd Never Speak Again*, teaches writing workshops online and in Santa Cruz, CA, and COVID permitting, leads transformative writing retreats around the world. In this time of pandemic, Laura sends out daily resources and has started a new weekly international writing class, Tuesdays with Laura: Writing Through the Pandemic. lauradavis.net

Carolyn Davis Rudolph. Writing is like prayer for me, touching into my truth. Feeding people healthy, sustainable food is my life's work. Organic farmers and fieldworkers are my heroes. Gratitude is my true religion and guides my actions. I adore being a 75-year-old woman, wife, mother and grandmother, committed to making noise and getting into good trouble.

Lisa DeSocio-Sweeney lives in Fresno, CA with her wife, Sharon. She loves her job as a nurse on the surgical floor at a local hospital and could not imagine doing anything else. Whenever she has a few days off, Lisa and Sharon head to their tiny house-on-wheels in Hollister, CA for rest and relaxation. Lisa is an avid bike rider who is training for AidsLifeCycle 2022.

Joan Donato: I am a Bostonian transplanted to California 35 years ago. Writing poetry is my avocation, along with teaching yoga. I enjoy walking with friends, studying Spanish, and travel, especially in Central America and Europe. I love playing with words and am excited to be involved with this literary adventure.

Marilyn DuHamel is a psychotherapist who lives on the edge of the wild in Ben Lomond, CA. Her writing appears in *Kosmos Journal, Dark Matter* and other publications. Marilyn's unwavering love and concern for the natural world sparked the creation of her blog, Earth Dialogues, at marilynduhamel.com.

Pamela Eakins, PhD, DD, CHT, is a Sociologist, Visionary Cosmologist, Mediator, Priestess, and Interfaith Minister near SF. She has taught at Stanford U and the U of Colorado. Her books include *Tarot of the Spirit, Lightning Papers, Visionary Cosmology,* and *Terra Nova*. She teaches and has a private practice, in-residence and on Zoom. Please visit her on YouTube. pamelaeakins.net, tarotofthespirit.com, pacificmysteryschool.com

Marigold Fine began writing at the kitchen table of her Chicago childhood. She enjoys integrating her love of storytelling, creativity and media. Marigold is a video producer/filmmaker since founding Full Circle Video Productions in 1984. She can be a goofball, plays well with others and always welcomes the muse.

Carolyn Brigit Flynn is writer and teacher, and the author of the poetry collection *Communion: In Praise of the Sacred Earth*. She edited the anthologies *Sacred Stone, Sacred Water: Women Writers and Artists Encounter Ireland,* and *Sisters Singing*. She is writing a memoir/history of Ireland, *The Light of Ordinary Days,* and teaches writing workshops in Santa Cruz, CA and Ireland. carolynbrigitflynn.com

Diane Frank is author of 8 poetry books, 3 novels, and a photo memoir of her 400-mile Himalaya trek. Her friends describe her as a harem of seven women in one very small body. She lives in the SF Bay Area where she dances, plays cello in the Golden Gate Symphony, and creates her life as an art form. Diane teaches at SF State U and Dominican U. *Blackberries in the Dream House,* her first novel, won the Chelson Award for Fiction and was nominated for the Pulitzer Prize. *Canon for Bears and Ponderosa Pines* received honors in the San Francisco Book Festival.

Sara Friedlander has lived in Santa Cruz and worked as a therapist, writer and artist for almost 50 years. She began photographing on her first trip abroad in 1969. Whether it's a single photograph or a mixed media collage, her intention is to honor her subject, be it an individual, nature or a sociopolitical struggle.

Terese Garcia is a writer and abstract artist born in Hollywood, CA in 1963. She holds a BA in Political Science from UCSB and attended Otis Parsons School of Art and Design, LA. Her art is nationally collected and exhibited; her poetry has been published and she continues to write manuscripts.

Finn Gratton is sad, angry, hoping, praying, listening, striving, singing, and surrendering in a tiny cabin in a yard full of flowers and vegetables and transitory animals in Santa Cruz, CA.

Dennis Hamilton, anthropologist, Unitarian minister, natural mystic, living in a call and response with the natural world. Buddhist practitioner, longtime student of psychedelics, outsider, intimate lover of Truth drenched in kindness.

Mary Kay Hamilton is a retired psychotherapist and cofounder of "The Society of Playful Spirits." She lives in Pacific Grove spending as much time as she can frolicking on the beach or exploring local forests. In her retirement she began quilting which in a few short years has progressed from innocent pastime to expensive obsession.

For many years, **Lawrie Hartt** has followed the guidance of the teachers, ancestors, and beings who have come in her dreams. A counselor, teacher and writer, she gathers circles of community rooted in learning to live in reciprocity with the natural world. In her earlier life she served as an Episcopal priest and trained as a classical pianist. While living in the city, she remains most at home in the wild.

Susan Heinz is a professional astrologer, artist and writer. She has been teaching archetypal astrology and giving in-depth personal consultations for 38 years. Susan teaches classes on Qabalah, the Tree of Life, and Tarot. With a BA in Fine Arts, she teaches ongoing expressive painting classes. Susan writes a monthly astrology article and has published her writing in *We'Moon Daily Guide.* susanheinz.com

Nancy Jones is a mixed media artist living and working in the rural, northern panhandle of Florida. Her work is infused with materials from nature that help carry messages about environmental and social impacts on our planet and also women's historic stories about these issues.

Sally Jones is a retired psychotherapist who relishes time to travel and share life with her partner, Dinah, their Yorkie, Trix, and her two children and four grandchildren. She keeps active by walking Trix while dancing to Johnny Cash, and riding her new e-trike. Sally's happiest when all her family can be together, which hasn't happened since November, 2019 when everyone celebrated her 80th birthday. She writes when she is inspired by life events.

Carol Kline's essay is from her blog at StreetwiseSpirituality.org, which is based on metaphysical information given in the form of lectures over a period of 30 years in Los Angeles. Former television reporter, producer, and writer, Carol is the author of *Streetwise Spirituality: 28 Days to Inner Fitness and Everyday Enlightenment.*

Nina Koocher has been on the earth a little over 70 years. In that time, she has traveled to 3 continents, 14 countries and 35 states. She has worked as a waitress, bookkeeper, educator, cinematographer, filmmaker, photographer and mother. Her films have won awards and screened in the US and abroad.

Jennifer Lagier has published eighteen books and also in *Fire and Rain: Ecopoetry of California; Missing Persons: Reflections on Dementia; ane Silent Screams: Poetic Journeys Through Addiction & Recovery*. Newest book: *Camille Comes Unglued* (CyberWit). Forthcoming: *Meditation on Seascapes and Cypress* (Blue Light Press). jlagier.net

Jan Landry teaches mindfulness practice with the intention to meet life with an open, kind heart and a curious mind. She writes to listen and tries to express the mystery found within everyday life. She is touched by our shared humanity and the relationship with the greater cosmos. jan@mindfulnessprograms.com

Kim Ly Bui is a Vietnamese American poet and retired librarian/community services director. Her poems have been published in feminist, environmental, sex positive, Southeast Asian and young adult anthologies. Kim finds hope in her bicultural heritage, the natural world and her grandchild's energetic sweetness.

Jean Mahoney is a poet who lives near the Pacific Ocean in Santa Cruz, CA. She has listened to the call of foghorns and the moon all her life.

Joanna Martin Listening to words crashing the jetty, humpbacks breaching the secrets of the sea, the murmur of mermaids in dreams, Joanna Martin began writing poetry over thirty years ago after she moved to Santa Cruz. Joanna has published two books of poetry with Hummingbird Press, *The Meaning of Wings* and *Where Stars Begin*. She has published poems in numerous literary magazines and anthologies including *Red Wheel Barrel, Porter Gulch Review, Harvest from the Emerald Orchard and phren-Z*.

Marda Messick: In this season of an elongating life, I'm a poet, neighbor, gardener and friend. In previous years I've also been a registered nurse, Lutheran pastor, and long-term caregiver. During the isolation of the pandemic I'm very grateful for poetry's power to mend and connect.

Deena Metzger lives at the end of the road in Topanga, CA where she writes, teaches and regularly gathers community, seeking to reawaken earth- and spirt-centered ways of living. Her latest books include *The Burden of Light, A Rain of Night Birds* and *La Negra y Blanca*, winner of an Oakland Pen Award for Literature. deenametzger.net.

Gail Newman A child of Polish Holocaust survivors, Gail was born in a Displaced Persons' Camp in Germany. Gail has worked as a poet-teacher for CalPoets, and arts administration and museum educator at the Contemporary Jewish Museum. Gail's poems have appeared in journals including *Nimrod International Journal, Prairie Schooner* and *Spillway* and in anthologies including *The Doll Collection, Ghosts of the Holocaust,* and *America, We Call Your Name.* Her poem "Mishpacha" was awarded first prize in the Bellingham Review 49th Parallel Poetry Contest. Gail was cofounder and editor of *Room, A Women's Literary Journal.* A book of poetry, *One World,* was published by Moon Tide Press. A new collection, *Blood Memory* (2020), was chosen by Marge Piercy for the Marsh Hawk Press Poetry Prize.

Robert Nielsen is a published poet, writer and photographer, whose home is in Carmel Valley, CA. Born in Australia, he has lived, worked, and traveled in many parts of the world. His poetry and photographs reflect his experience, perceptions, feelings and dreams; each can be read or seen on its own, or together as parts of a larger story. Formerly an international lawyer, an artist always, he stays balanced by cultivating his own garden, namely his heart, voice and vision. pilgrim-arts.com

Cassidy Parong is a dancer, a dreamer, and perhaps most of all a lover of language. Her passion for community rights has led her to pursue projects in language preservation and revitalization. By using a multidisciplinary approach, she hopes to ground awareness and activism in embodied movement and poetic experimentation.

Maggie Paul is the author of *Borrowed World,* (Hummingbird Press 2011), *Scrimshaw* (Hummingbird Press 2020), and the chapbook, *Stones from the Baskets of Others* (Black Dirt Press 2000). Her poetry, reviews, and interviews have appeared in *Catamaran, Rattle, Monterey Poetry Review, Porter Gulch Review, Red Wheelbarrow, phren-Z, SALT,* and others. She is an education consultant and writing instructor in Santa Cruz, CA. For more information: maggiepaulpoetry. com; myessaycoach.com; dasulliv1.wixsite.com/ hummingbirdpress

Clem Peterson is a young poet, currently in their second year at Cabrillo College. They have been published in *Porter Gulch Review* and contributed to multiple local poetry anthologies and contests. When Clem was rejected from kindergarten they taught themself how to read and write and since then has been continuing to create while being alarmingly fascinated by birds, silhouettes and hammocking.

Dan Phillips, long-time word conjurer, tempts local ears and poetic palates with publications in the *Porter Gulch Review, Catamaran, phren-Z, Homestead Review* and *Monterey Poetry Review.* Poetry books include *Coastlines: Eight Santa Cruz Poets, Places of the Spirit* and a memoir in poetry and prose, *The Bali in Me.*

Judy Phillips is preparing to enter her eighth decade by letting her hair go gray, finishing her memoir, and making peace with herself while raging against the dying of the light.

Jory Post is a writer, artist, and educator. His first book of prose poetry, *The Extra Year,* was published by Anaphora Literary Press in 2019, followed by *Of Two Minds* in 2020. His work has been published in *Catamaran, Chicago Quarterly Review, Rumble Fish Quarterly, The Sun,* and elsewhere. His short stories "Sweet Jesus" and "Hunt and Gather" were nominated for the 2019 Pushcart Prize.

Bernice Rendrick lives and writes poetry in Scotts Valley, CA. She misses The Library Poetry Circle and the Senior Center, and recently had a new adventure when she and her daughter were evacuated from the fires. She has published poetry in *Red Wheelbarrow*, *phren-Z*, and many magazines and journals.

Eva Rider MA, MFT is a Jungian-oriented depth psychotherapist, workshop leader and presenter. She has taught in the US and Canada and teaches internationally online. Eva's teaching incorporates poetry and dreamwork with fairytale, myth, tarot, music, dance and collage, based in exploring correspondences between Jungian theory, alchemy and psyche/soma through the Hermetic tree of life. She is a graduate of McGill U and John F. Kennedy U, where she taught as adjunct instructor. Eva is a certified hypnotherapist, Movement-Expression® teacher, SoulCollage® facilitator and TRE® practitioner.

Sarojani Rohan, retired from teaching, is a published poet and part-time musician. She lives in the Santa Cruz mountains with her husband, writes, draws, and is often found staring googly-eyed at pictures of her new grandson. She believes in a coming age filled with reverence for all life. She has often been accused of asking too many questions...and wistfully wonders what it would be like to be an investigative journalist.

Donna Runnalls is a psychotherapist, Qi Gong Teacher, and directs a nonprofit she founded in 1994, Living Bridges Foundation, to fund and support threatened environments and peoples in the Southern Americas. She has spent many months in the rainforests and mountains of Peru and Ecuador and has a lifelong love of the Natural World.

Jan Rupp I was born in Santa Cruz, CA, where the natural environment put its stamp on me early in life. I moved back with my husband in 1977 and we raised our two children there. I brought with me many beautiful memories of life in Yosemite, traveling, and the inner growth one experiences within a decade of life. I competed a Masters in Education via Bethany U, a capstone to 35 years of working with elementary schoolchildren. Santa Cruz continues to be a place of inspiration where the creative arts abound and I feel blessed daily to live here.

Nora Sarkissian A native of MA, I lived in San Francisco, Germany, London England, Rhode Island and Colorado, and settled in Santa Cruz CA for the past 30 years. I attended Rudolf Steiner College, Chrysalis Acting School in London, and was a Potters Apprentice in Germany. I received BAs from the Naropa Institute in Boulder, and the U of Massachusetts, and an MFA at SJSU. I have been in writing groups for the past 15 years. I worked with Coeleen Kiebert at UCSC and have a certificate in Expressive Art Therapy from Salve Regina U. I taught ceramic sculpture to kids and adults for many years through SPECTRA and Art Centers in the Bay Area and in my studio. I currently exhibit ceramic sculpture at SFWA.

Linda Serrato was born in LA, grew up in SF and now lives in Chico, CA. She holds a BA in Liberal Studies from CSU Chico and an MA in Creative Writing from SF State U Her poems have been published in *Sisters Singing; Sacred Stone, Sacred Water; Travelogue for Two: Poems by Sanford and Friends;* and several issues of *Watershed Literary Review.* She is a retired elementary school teacher and has taught bilingual classes in Salinas and dual immersion classes in Chico. Things that keep her grounded in these uncertain times: her grandchildren and children, friends, walking, art, humor, the gifts of nature and prayer.

Mariabruna Sirabella Born in Italy, adopted by India, naturalized in the US, Mariabruna is an avid traveler and nature lover who upholds creativity and visioning as primary tools for soul empowerment. She teaches internationally, drawing from 30 years of passionate research and facilitation of SoulCollage® and of her School of the Origins. mariabruna.com

Anne Stafford-Wade Formerly living in Santa Cruz and recently relocated to LA, Anne has authored and published a popular children's book, *Dogs at the Beach*, and is at work on a second. She has written professionally and personally for many years, and wishes to thank her writing group and guide Carolyn Brigit Flynn for supporting and helping her find her poetic voice.

Ratna Jennifer (Jenna) Sturz felt drawn to Santa Cruz while passing through on a summer road trip and moved here in '74. She enjoys being active outdoors in this beautiful coastal area. Ratna is close to finishing her longtime project, *Drink from Her Well*. Her coaching practice supports people on their life path.

David Allen Sullivan is poet laureate of Santa Cruz County, California. His books include *Strong-Armed Angels, Every Seed of the Pomegranate, Bombs Have Not Breakfasted Yet*, and *Black Ice*. He won the Mary Ballard Chapbook poetry prize for *Take Wing*, and his book of poems about the year he spent as a Fulbright lecturer in China, *Seed Shell Ash*, is forthcoming from Salmon Press. *Nightjars*, a long narrative poem about the friendship between an Iraqi interpreter and a US soldier, is searching for a home. The first section won the *Golden Walkman* aural chapbook award and is available as a podcast. David teaches at Cabrillo College, where he edits the *Porter Gulch Review* with his students. He lives in Santa Cruz with his family. His poetry website is dasulliv1.wixsite.com/website-1, a modern Chinese co-translation project is at dasulliv1.wixsite.com/website-trans, and he's searching for a publisher for an anthology of poetry about the paintings of Bosch and Bruegel he edited with his art historian mother, who died recently.

Barbara Thomas is a painter, writer, and faithful liaison between the worlds of angels, nature spirits, and humans. Drawn by destiny, teachers and guides, trainings and pilgrimages led her to her core task of working intimately with the angels and nature spirits on her land in the Santa Cruz Mountains. Besides many paintings, Barbara is the author of *Celebrating the Magic of Jim's Road* and *Living with the Spirits of the Land*, and the Council of Gnomes Blog: A Collaboration (barbarathomas.info/blog).

Mary Camille Thomas is a native of Santa Cruz who considers herself lucky to have returned after several years living in Davis, Germany, LA, Holland, and on the road in a motorhome. A librarian by profession, she blogs at "The Kingdom of Enough" and is working on a novel called *Schatz*.

Cynthia Travis is a writer and photographer. She is currently writing a family memoir that is also a natural history of empire. Her blog, "Earth Altar," features Full and New Moon posts chronicling intimate personal encounters with the natural world (earth-altar.org). She lives on the Mendocino Coast in Northern CA.

Bill Underwood resides in Santa Cruz CA, where he enjoys the outdoors, photography, biking, cooking and spontaneously writing down the bones of his heartfelt moments. He spends much of his day as a leadership coach helping people bring more of themselves into their living.

Poet, nonfiction writer, and teacher **Patrice Vecchione**'s new book, *My Shouting, Shattered, Whispering Voice: A Guide to Writing Poetry & Speaking Your Truth* was published in 2020. Kirkus Reviews called it "At once impassioned and practical poetic advice." Her other books include, most recently, *Ink Knows No Borders: Poems of the Immigrant and Refugee Experience* and *Step into Nature: Nurturing Imagination and Spirit in Everyday Life*. She's the author of two collections of poetry and the editor of many anthologies. Adrienne Rich called her, "One of those stead, vibrant, serious and passionate temperaments who continually replenish our sense of communal creativity." Find out about Patrice's writing workshops at patricevecchione.com.

barbara j weigel ... woman, mother, grandmother, friend, dog person, artist, swimmer, writer, and natural philosopher. i find inspiration in the known and unknown process of living each day.

Deborah Wenzler is a creative test writer, editor, world traveler and chef. Her poetry has appeared in *The Atlanta Review, Immagine* and *Poesia* and *Song of the San Joaquin.* In 2019, Deborah published *Well Beyond the Water,* Book I of her poetic trilogy, *Messages from the Deep.* She hopes to complete Book II, *Love is the "O,"* in mid-2021.

Anne Ylvisaker is a Monterey artist and author of several children's novels. Her current projects include *Surprised by Delight,* poems and images based on daily observation of her immediate world, a practice that brings her hope in hard times. She is also at work on a novel-in-verse.

Karen Zelin is a Santa Cruz resident, and a teacher and student of meditation and yoga. She is grateful to be a part of Santa Cruz's wonderful subculture of artists and writers—many of whom have been seen lately on Zoom. Deep bows to all the teachers who've been bringing us all along.

Made in the USA
Coppell, TX
02 November 2020